AMERICAN LITERATURE

Studies on Emerson, Thoreau, Hawthorne, Melville and Whitman

Sujata Gurudev

ATLANTIC
PUBLISHERS & DISTRIBUTORS (P) LTD

ATLANTIC
PUBLISHERS & DISTRIBUTORS (P) LTD

7/22, Ansari Road, Darya Ganj, New Delhi
Tel.: +91-11-4077 5252, 2327 3880
E-mail: orders@atlanticbooks.com
Web: www.atlanticbooks.com

Reprint 2026, 2024, 2011

Published by Atlantic Publishers & Distributors (P) Ltd.

Printed & bound in India by Atlantic Print Services

Preface

American Literature: Studies on Emerson, Thoreau, Hawthorne, Melville, and Whitman attempts to bring before the reading public an in-depth analysis of the literary scenario of nineteenth-century America—an era unique in the flowering of diverse literary talents, from men of letters like Emerson and Thoreau to novelists like Hawthorne and Melville, to the prophetic vision of Whitman.

The period being one of the richest in American history, saw the flowering of a rare breed of Humanism where an all -out attempt was made to understand the egoistic and altruistic motives in man. Transcendentalism was the crowning glory of such an attempt. While the dark shadow of Puritanism cast over Hawthorne's fiction an uneasy shadow, Melville passionately denounced in fictional terms the duplicity of what he termed as 'Divine Depravity'. Whitman celebrated the word en-masse or the Divine Average. Thoreau, likewise, walked past the Walden Pond with a naturalistic zeal attempting to come to terms with "nature red in tooth and claw".

The book attempts to wade through a bewildering literary maze in an attempt to highlight not merely the literary figures of the age, their celebrated works, but also the reasons behind the flowering of their genius. Replete with in-depth critical research, the works of Emerson, Thoreau, Hawthorne, Melville and Whitman are presented to contemporary readers.

Sujata Gurudev

Contents

Introduction: The American Dream

The eastern nations sink, their glory ends,
And empire rises where the sun descends.

—The Plymouth Rock Verses

Gilbert Chinard, speaking of the American Dream, affirms that "as a State of mind and a dream, America had existed long before its discovery."[1] Ever since the early days of Western civilization people had dreamt of a Lost Paradise, a new Eden, a Golden age characterized by abundance and a lack of sweat and oil.

The discovery of the New World was in keeping with the idyllic myths of the Lost World, whether it is the Greek idea of Elysian fields or the Roman Islands of the Blest. So great was the ideological fervour generated by the discovery of the New World, that Columbus (on his third voyage of exploration to America) felt that he had located the Terrestrial Paradise. Thus, the New World seemed to promise mankind a new Adam, a return to innocence and joy, as well as freedom from care and labour, a journey back to Eden.

The euphoria somewhat diminished when the early colonists came to terms with the harsh reality of America. By the mid-sixteenth century, Europeans no longer associated the New World with the age of gold but with a land of gold. The Spanish made inroads to America to subjugate the natives and divest them of their treasures.

The English colonists were disappointed in their early attempts to find colonies. Despite repeated failures, the English continued to have great expectations of America. Michael

Drayton, an English poet writing in the 17th century, in his poem "To the Virginian Voyage", not only celebrates the English colonization attempt but also combines the vision of a Land of Gold with traditional ideas of empire and heaven,

And cheerefully at Sea,
Success you still intice,
To get the Pearl and Gold,
And ours to hold,
Virginia
Earth's only Paradise.[2]

The first permanent colonists in America settled at Jamestown, Virginia, in 1607. The reasons behind the emigration to America are varied. The Virginia Company of London, which sponsored the settlement certainly expected economic profit. The early colonists were expected to add greater glory and power to the Crown. While emigrants hoped for success in terms of gold, what they found was timber, fish, furs and tobacco—the real sources of American wealth. In 1618, the Virginia Company began giving fifty acres of land to every individual who transported himself to America. Thus, the future of American colonization was secured. The freehold system of grants of land was responsible for peopling America.

Captain John Smith, who sailed with the first colonists to Virginia in 1607, saw America primarily as a land of opportunity. In *A Description of New England* (1616), he affirms, "who can desire more content, that hath small meanes; or but only his merit to advance his fortune, than to tread, and plant that ground he hath purchased by the hazard of his life?"[3] Another motive for the mass emigration to America was religious emancipation. The great Puritan migration to Massachusetts Bay took place in 1630, and the Catholic settlement of Maryland in 1633. Roger William's refuge in Rhode Island was established in 1636 and William Penn's Quaker colony in Pennsylvania in 1682.

John Winthrop, who preached "A Model of Christian Charity" on board the 'Arabella,' the flagship of the great Puritan migration to Massachusetts in 1630, felt that America would become a world model: "We shall find that the God in Israel is among us, when ten of us shall be able to resist a thousand of our enemies; when he shall make us a praise and glory that men shall say of succeeding plantations, 'The Lord make it like that of New England' for we must consider that we shall be a City upon a hill."[4] Winthrop meant that the New England puritans would establish a religious way of life which would lead the world into the millennium. Winthrop felt that the puritans had entered into a covenant with God. If God "ratified this covenant" by bringing them safely to America, then God would expect "a strict performance of the Articles contained in it". He felt that the New England community would be one of love where everyone would identify with and delight in one another, share in each other's joys and sorrows, and pray together.

Besides the religious factor and the economic lure of America, social conditions in Europe aided emigration. America provided an asylum for refugees the world over. It attracted the "cream and scum" of society. It was in America that Coleridge planned to establish his pantisocracy. It was the land where Robert Owen, after his unsuccessful experiment in England, came to build his New Harmony and where the German Rapp established his communistic village of Economy, sixteen miles from Pittsburgh. The Napoleonic exiles, after Waterloo, had come as "Soldier farmers" with General Bertrand to plant "the vine and the olive" in the wilds of Texas and Alabama.

America was the only country on earth where the French Socialist Cabet could organize colonies of Icarians, because nowhere else could small groups, advocates of a new order, establish and govern themselves locally and practically without any interference from a central government. It was a land where Priestley and Thomas Cooper from England, General Bertrand, Jerome Bonaparte, and Achille Murat after the fall of Napoleon, had found asylum. It was a land where the Germans, the Irish and the French, after 1848, came as refugees to seek liberty, which they despaired of establishing in their own countries. It was a "melting pot" of diverse cultures, traditions, and people.

In addition, it was a land of hope. Louis Hartz, in *The Liberal Tradition in America* (1955) analyses the perspectives of 1776, the mood of the age, the sense of Utopia— "when the Americans celebrated the uniqueness of their own society, they were on the track of personal insight of the profoundest importance. For the non-feudal world in which they lived shaped every aspect of their social thought, it gave them a frame of mind that cannot be found anywhere else in the eighteenth century, or in the wider history of modern revolution."[5] Representatives from all the nations of the world, thinkers, reformers, and poets were called upon to play their part in this "Commonwealth of Nations." As testified by the International Peace Conference under Victor Hugo in 1848, the American people were not a 'bunch' of wild dreamers.

The United States of America validates Hegel's chief axiom, that unity dominates the diversity of elements. The United States symbolized hope that the people of the Old World could be redeemed from themselves. St. John de Crevecoeur, the French intellectual, celebrates the Epic heroism of the American frontier man. In *Letters from an American Farmer* (1782), he amply qualifies the term American:

> Here individuals of all nations are melted into a new race of men, whose labours and posterity will one day cause great changes in the world. Americans are the Western pilgrims who are carrying along with them that great mass of arts, sciences, vigour, and industry which began long since in the East; they finish the great circle...the American is a new man, who acts upon new principles; he must therefore entertain new ideas and form new opinions. From involuntary idleness, servile dependence, penury, and useless labour, he has passed the toils of a very different nature, rewarded by ample subsistence. This is an American.[6]

Thus, the American Dream, from rags to riches, the Horatio Algiers myth became a part of the European tradition.

At the time of the Revolution, American Liberals were imbued with European ideals, during the early years of the Republic, Conservatives were equally willing to accept foreign thought. However, a new generation soon grew up that adjusted Old World concepts to their own activities and began to create indigenous symbols to represent their own experiences. Out of this ferment, there emerged a new way of life dominated by the twin forces of 'self-trust' and 'expansion.'

Expansion in the American context implied 'Manifest destiny' a phrase used by contemporaries and historians to describe the continental expansion of the United States in the 1840s. It implied that the United States was destined by the will of Heaven to become a country of political and territorial eminence. Manifest destiny suggested that the American people were destined to extend their democratic principles over the North American continent. The Texas annexation became a political issue in 1844. This was followed by the national debate over Oregon in 1845. California, no less than Oregon, demanded its own peculiar expansionist rationale. A fact amply demonstrated by Polk's War for California Polk adequately supported by the Democratic expansionists in Congress rationalized the American retention of California, not with references to the doctrine of regeneration, but with the principle of indemnity. Mexico had to pay the price. Finally, expansionists ratified the annexation of Mexico because it was humane. Military occupation of Mexico was justified since it saved her from the uncontrolled dominance of barbarians who oppressed her. As late as 1859, James Buchanan sparked another bust of expansion towards Cuba, but without the physical coercion of Spain, it remained an impossible dream.

Expansion gave the American nation a profound sense of purpose. John L. O'Sullivan in his essay "The Great Nation of Futurity" (1839) affirmed:

> We are the nation of human progress, and who will, what can, set limits to our onward march? Providence is with us,...the far-reaching, the boundless future will be the era of American greatness. In its magnificent domain of space and time, the nation of many nations is destined to manifest the excellence of divine principles; to establish on earth the noblest temple ever dedicated to the worship of the Most High—The Sacred and the True.[7]

Thus, expansion and the concept of self-trust held the American nation together as one people. Myra Jehlen, in the *American*

Incarnation (1986), points out that "to be born an American is simultaneously to be born again. Americans assume their national identity as the fulfillment of selfhood rather than as its point of origin, so that they travel their lives in a state of perpetual landing."[8] Thus, there are two processes at work in the making of an American. He is the Adamic man alone in the wilderness. Inspired by the land's physical emanations, the abstract individual becomes an American, and as an American he is not merely singular but representative. The representativeness of the autonomous individual provides a basis for a community. Myra Jehlen explicates "since it is by being autonomous that each man thus connects to others, he remains free, in fact becomes free in connection. But the connection is not therefore less adhesive. Where others have found an absence, I see on the contrary, the powerful presence of a civilization conceived to be inherent in nature, springing forth coeval with each American as an organic part of his individuality."[9] This unity in diversity found its way into the utterances of Clay, Webster, and Calhoun. In this cross-current of ideas, the generation of Lincoln and Emerson came to maturity. However, neither the general confidence nor the manifold promises of the period can alone explain the peak reached by American Literature during the nineteenth century.

The third more decisive contributing factor besides self-trust and expansion was the re-orientation of literature under the influence of New England Transcendentalism. Its exponents were a small group of New England intellectuals who, after rejecting both Rationalism and Calvinism, built their own faith around the divinity of man. Their nucleus was the informal transcendental club, their organ was the Dial, and their most influential spokesmen were William Ellery Channing and Ralph Waldo Emerson.

Channing announced the fundamental principles of Transcendentalism. God as all-loving and all-pervading, the presence of this God in all men makes them divine, and the true worship of God is goodwill to all men. Emerson elaborated its individualistic tendencies by stressing intuition, platonic idealism, and self-reliance. Transcendentalism conferred upon American

Literature a perspective far wider and deeper than proposed by its own formulated doctrines, the perspective of humanity itself.

This perspective gives common purpose and meaning to the otherwise divergent achievements of Emerson, Thoreau, Hawthorne, Melville, and Whitman. An in-depth analysis of the humanistic perspective in the writings of these literary figures has been the focal point of this work. The prerequisite for such an analysis would naturally be a just appreciation of the term "Humanism."

Humanism is basically a system of education based on the Greek and Roman Classics. Arthur Hazard Dakin in *Man The Measure: An Essay on Humanism as Religion* (1939) states that "for sophists generally, as for Protagoras in particular, the proper study of mankind was man—the measure of all things, in the sense that anything beyond his immediate concern and common grasp was a matter of indifference."[10] It also refers to a set of attitudes that accompanied the end of the middle ages and was represented at different periods by the Renaissance, the Reformation, the Industrial Revolution and the struggle for Democracy. These include "release from ecclesiastical authority, the liberation of the intellect, faith in progress, the belief that man himself can improve his own conditions without supernatural help and, indeed has a duty to do so."[11] 'Man is the measure of all things' is the keynote of humanism. The humanist has faith in man's intellectual and spiritual resources to bring knowledge and understanding to the world. Among the fundamental moral principles, he would count those of freedom, justice, tolerance and happiness. Thus, in its wider connotation as a set of attitudes, the term humanism or its corollary, the humanistic perspective, would be equally applicable to the five great American writers—Emerson, Thoreau, Hawthorne, Melville, and Whitman. Common to these writers as to all great writers, is a profound sense of the human predicament. The questions that beset man as man, and of the relation of these problems to man's defects and potentialities. Thus, all these writers share a common framework of ideas within which they seek to understand the problem of man. The framework or perspective in all instances is radically humanistic. Further, the perspective shared alike by these writers is also universalized. The emphasis is not upon man in particular as a European or American but upon man as universal, freed from the accidents of time and space, and reduced to his common humanity.

Keeping the humanistic perspective in mind, a further assumption common to all five writers is the belief that individual virtue and happiness depend upon self-realization. Self-realization implying a harmonious blend of the altruistic and egoistic motivations in the self. Emerson, Thoreau, Hawthorne, Melville, and Whitman agree upon self-realization as an ethical ideal but disagree on how this ideal can be actualized. Hawthorne and Melville doubt whether a genuine harmony between the individual and his cosmos is possible, finally common to all five writers is the belief that the organic relationship between the self and the cosmos can only be realized by the power of intuition and imagination, faith in the imagination enabled Emerson, Thoreau, Hawthorne, Melville, and Whitman to realize their own moral and metaphysical insights. This also accounts for their conception of the writer as a seer and the deeply humanistic thrust of their living.

Having indicated the crucial importance of the American dream, self-trust, expansion, and transcendentalism as formative influences leading to the humanistic perspective in the writings of Emerson, Thoreau, Hawthorne, Melville, and Whitman, the chapters that follow shall highlight each writer's attitude to man.

This finds expression in transcendental terms in Emerson, in terms of romantic naturalism in Thoreau, in psychological terms in Hawthorne and Melville and finally in prophetic terms in Whitman. Taken collectively it would imply "The Song of Man" or the vision of an anthropocentric universe.

End Notes

1. Robert E. Spiller, ed., *Literary History of the United States* (New York: MacMillan Publishing Co., 1946), 196.
2. Michael Drayton, *Poems, Lyrics and Pastorals.*
3. Edward Arber and A.C. Bradley, eds., *A Description of New England* (1616): *Travels and Works of Captain John Smith* (Edinburgh: John Grant, 1910), 207-11.

4. Stewart Mitchell, Allyn Bailey Forbes, eds., *The Winthrop Papers,* 5 vols. (Boston: Massachusetts Historical Society, 1929-47), 2: 282-95.
5. Louis Hartz, *The Liberal Tradition in America* (New York: Harcourt, Brace and Company, 1955), 35-66.
6. St. John de Creve coeur, *Letters from an American Farmer,* ed. Albert E. Stone (New York: Penguin, 1981), 66-105.
7. John L. O'Sullivan, "The Great Nation of Futurity," *The United States Magazine and Democratic Review*, VI (November, 1839), 426-430.
8. Myra Jehlan, *American Incarnation*: *The Individual, the Nation and the Continent* (Harvard University Press, Cambridge, Massachusetts and London, England, 1986), 1-42.
9. *Ibid.*, 15.
10. Arthur Hazard Dakin, *Man The Measure*: *An Essay on Humanism as Religion* (Princeton: Princeton University Press, 1939), 23.
11. Christopher Cook, ed., *Pears Encyclopaedia,* (Kensington: Pelham Books, 1986-87).

1

Emerson: Man Thinking

I will not live out of me
I will not see with other's eyes
My good is good, my evil ill
I would be free; I cannot be
While I take things as others please to rate them.
I dare attempt to lay out my road.
That which myself delights in shall be good,
That which I do not want, indifferent;
That which I hate is Bad, that's flat.

—R.W. Emerson

Emerson was his own "Man Thinking." He brought into focus the full meaning of two centuries of life on the Atlantic Seaboard of America. He did this in two ways. Firstly, by carrying to its ultimate statement the individuals' revolt from authority marked the transition from the medieval world to modern. Secondly, by formulating the dichotomy between the vision of Jonathan Edwards and the common sense of Benjamin Franklin, a conflict and balance vital to American life.

Emerson's logic and metaphysics remained without a system. His art, like that of all great American Romantics, retained its organic freedom. The discussion on Emerson will attempt to explore through his writings his unique vision of man. Keeping in mind his transcendental bias, "man" is basically the "transcendental man."

The movement that came to be called Transcendentalism originated in a conflict within the communion of Boston-Unitarianism. Boston Unitarianism in the first third of the nineteenth century was an exquisite socio-theological creation. By the beginning of the nineteenth century, the principle doctrines of Unitarianism had been hammered out and required only a confident and unified interpretation. This was finally achieved in the work of William Ellery Channing, the spokesman of Unitarianism's Golden Age from 1819, when he delivered his discourse at the ordination of Jared Sparks ('Unitarian Christianity') to his death in 1841. Thus, he laid the foundation for the formal Liberal Unitarian creed and called in question the Calvinistic theory about the depravity of human nature.

Channing began with a typical eighteenth-century insistence on the rationality of the Christian religion and the perfect adequacy of human reason to interpret its meaning. The *Bible* was a book written for men in the language of men. Man was perfectly capable of interpreting and assimilating its contents, nor was man a wholly depraved creature, his reason so dreadfully darkened by Adam's fall so as to render him unworthy of salvation. Channing sternly indicted old-line Calvinism:

> We object...to that system, which arrogates to itself the name of orthodoxy and which is now industriously propagated through our country. According to its old and genuine forms, it teaches that God brings us into life wholly depraved, so that under the innocent features of our childhood is hidden, a nature averse to all good and propense to all evil, a nature which exposes us to God's displeasure and wrath, even before we have acquired power to understand our duties, or to reflect upon our actions....We come from the hands of our Maker, with such a constitution, and are placed under such influences and circumstances, as to render certain and infallible the total depravity of every human being, from the first moment of his moral agency.[1]

Channing further avowed that man's reasonable nature was a fundamental ground of unity with God. Christ was the model of perfection towards which he could aim. By the light of reason, man could approximate the divine character. "When do we derive our knowledge of the attributes and perfections which constitute the Supreme Being? I answer we derive them from our own souls. The divine attributes are first developed in ourselves and thence transferred to our creator. The idea of God, sublime and awful as it is, is the idea of our own spiritual nature, purified and enlarged to infinity. In ourselves are the elements of the Divinity."[2] However, having come to the verge of Transcendental heresy, Channing was unable to take a step further and qualify the 'elements' within man that were wholly identified with the Divine. This was partially due to the fact that his assumptions of human reason were grounded in Locke's epistemology and further that he recoiled from any brand of Pantheism. Thus, it was left to young Emerson to carry Unitarian Liberalism to its ultimate statement and blaze forth the tenets of Transcendentalism.

The early sermons of Emerson did not depart radically from Channing and were concerned with the old impasse of Trinitarianism versus Unitarianism and the Divinity of Christ. However, in "A Feast of Remembrance", Emerson hinted at his dissatisfaction with the ritual of the Lord's Supper as administered at the Second Church in Boston; an issue over which he resigned his pastorate in 1832. In spite of various personal disasters, Emerson found himself thrust into the larger world of nineteenth-century thought—scientific, philosophical and aesthetic in the brilliant decade of the thirties.

Kenneth Walter Cameron, in *Young Emerson's Transcendental Vision* (1836), sums up the world background to the period (1775-1849). It was a period of reform movements, revolutions and democratic upheavals coloured by optimism about man's possibilities and perfectibility. The Industrial Revolution gave rise to a concept of progressive materialism. Fourier and Proudhon sought to combat it with experiments in socialism. Transcendentalists experimented with collectivism at Brook Farm and Fruitlands. Thoreau, however, kept aloof from collectivism, preferring individualism. Aesthetically, the age inclined towards

Romanticism, which in turn preferred the Dionysian to the Apollonian.

Conventional spirituality was at a low ebb. On the one hand, there was the aridity of eighteenth-century Deism, and on the other, the disintegration of Calvinism. In a lecture to the Concord Lyceum (1880), Emerson qualified the spirit of the times:

> It seemed a war between the intellect and affectation; a crack in nature, which split every church in Christendom into Papal and Protestant, Calvinism into Old and New Schools, Quakerism into Old and New, brought new divisions in politics; as the new conscience touching temperance and slavery. The key to the period appeared to be that the mind had become aware of itself. Men grew reflective and intellectual. There was a new consciousness. The former generations acted upon the belief that a shining social prosperity was the beatitude of man, and sacrificed uniformly the citizen to the state. The modern mind believed that the nation existed for the individual, for the guardianship and education of every man. This idea, roughly written in revolutions and national movements, in the mind of the philosopher had far more precision; the individual is the World.[3]

Emerson realised that the root of intellectual evil in their time was Lockean empiricism. In seeking a way out of the Lockean impasse, he concluded that Reason was not simply a mode of thinking but a fact of consciousness that required a complete redefinition of the nature of man. When the Transcendentalists spoke of a "universal soul within or behind individual life" or of "the divine spirit in man", they were attempting a redefinition.

This took the Transcendentalists, as also Emerson, way beyond Channing and the formal theology of the Harvard Divinity School. They realised that God was in man, that man was "a God in ruins" albeit waiting to be resurrected. The immediacy of the individual soul to the divine order of the universe was a premise from which Emerson never departed and provided the background to his vision of the "Transcendental Man":

> There is no chance and no anarchy in the universe. All is system and gradation. Every God is there sitting in his sphere. The young mortal enters the hall of the firmament; there is he alone with them alone, they pouring on him benedictions and gifts, and beckoning him up to their thrones. On the instant, and incessantly, fall snow-storms of illusions. He fancies himself in a vast crowd which says this way and that and whose movements and doings he must obey; he fancies himself poor, orphaned, insignificant. The mad crowd drives hither and thither, now furiously commanding this thing to be done, now that. What is he that he should resist their will, and think and act for himself. Every moment new changes and new shower of deceptions to baffle and distract him and when, by and by, for an instant, the air clears and the cloud lifts a little, there are the Gods still around him on their thrones—they alone with him alone.[4] ('Illusions', 1860)

Since the divinity of man was the central metaphor of the Transcendentalists, it was left to Emerson to isolate and qualify the faculty within man, which would help him realise his goal. This Emerson called Reason (spelt with a capital R to distinguish it from the eighteenth-century version). It was, essentially, the American version of the great Romantic rediscovery of the intuitive and creative powers of the mind. Emerson borrowed the idea from Coleridge, while Brownson Alcott got his version from Cousin, who in turn derived it from post-Kantian German philosophy.

In order to get a better understanding of the term 'Reason' as opposed to 'understanding', Emerson formulated what he called the 'Laws of the first philosophy'—an essential pre-requisite which awakens in man the feeling of the 'moral sublime.' The first philosophy of mind is the science of what 'is' in distinction from what 'appears.' Further, that "our compound nature differences us from God, but our Reason is not to be distinguished from the divine essence."[5] Emerson felt that man was conscious of a "two-fold nature" which manifested itself in perpetual self-contradiction.

To represent this duality the English philosophers distinguished between Reason and Understanding. Emerson asserts that "Reason is the superior principle." Its attributes are eternity and intuition. "We belong to it, not it to us." The understanding, on the other hand, is the executive faculty. "It mediates between the soul and inert matter. It works in time and space and therefore successively. It divides, compares, reasons, and invents. It lives from the Reason yet disobeys it. It commands the material world, yet often for the pleasure of the sense."[6] Thus, Emerson was aware of the polarity in man. Pure Reason, with its attributes of 'God, Justice, Free Will, Necessity, War and Intellectual Reason' had to come to terms with practical common sense and mercantile values. The mystic had to co-exist with the Yankee. The true transcendental man was one who unified within himself this duality.

Having qualified the attributes of Reason, the Transcendentalists believed that it would lead to the liberated Individual: "Jesus Christ was a minister of pure Reason." Even so, every individual had the potential. Thus, the Transcendentalists called for the liberation of mankind. They traced the cause of his bondage to society, to the mass of forms and conventions and institutions by which men were held captive and alienated from their true selves.

Emerson thus places self-reliance at the very centre of his theory of man. In his book *The Power and Form of Emerson's Thought* (1973), Jeffrey L. Duncan elucidates that the whole is in each man and is the source of the worth of each man:

> Self-reliance is Emerson's interpretation of the sentences of Luke—"The Kingdom of God is within you"—and Paul "We are the temple of the Living God." He emphasises throughout his career that the reliance should be placed in that which is the cause; that as an effect a man should never lose sight of the truth, that he did not create himself, that he is a manifestation of powers not his own, and that he therefore should never transfer his reliance to himself as an effect...such a transfer is the fall, the disease of the will, rebellion and separation from the eternal to which he feels every man properly belongs.[7]

Thus, the Transcendental man should be a self-reliant man, *i.e.*, a man should learn to detect and watch for "that gleam of light which flashes across his mind from within more than the lustre of the firmament of bards and sages."[8] There is, according to Emerson, a special "power" within every man that should be made manifest: "Trust Thyself: every heart vibrates to that iron string. Accept the place the divine providence has found for you." Man is bound by convention, tradition and the opinion of his peers. He is, as it were, "clapped into jail" by his consciousness. Thus, he remains in a passive, inert state, chained by fear and neutrality. The gaoler or villain of the piece that denies man his freedom is society— "Society everywhere is in conspiracy against the manhood of every one of its members. Society is a joint stock company, in which the members agree for the better securing of his bread to each shareholder, to surrender the liberty and culture of the eater."[9] Thus, in order to be a man (a Transcendental man), one has to be a non-conformist. One has to live and die by one's values.

Emerson's belief in the intrinsic value and worth of man leads him to the radical stance of asserting, "The only right is what is after my constitution, the only wrong is that is against it." However, this should not be misinterpreted as license: the right to do as one pleases. The Transcendental man was not any man. He belonged to a particular class. He was not a virtuous man or a "do-gooder," the average philanthropist given to every charitable cause. In his essay "Self-Reliance," Emerson squarely asserts "I grudge the dollar, the dime, the cent I give to such men as do not belong to me and to whom I do not belong. There is a class of persons to whom, by all spiritual affinity, I am bought and sold; for them I will go to prison if need be."[10] Thus the Transcendental man is not known by his actions:

> I ask primary evidence that you are a man, and refuse this appeal from man to his actions. Such a man does not possess the "herd-instinct." Nor does he keep aloof in Solitary isolation. Rather he has a balanced character, "It is easy in the World to live after the World's opinion; it is easy in solitude to live after our own; but the great man

> is he who in the midst of the crowd keeps with perfect sweetness the independence of solitude.[11]

Self-reliance, being true to one's nature, leads to the advent of the Spheral man, "I suppose no man can violate his own nature. All the sallies of his will are rounded in by the law of his being, as the inequalities of the Andes and Himmaleh are insignificant in the curve of the sphere."[12] Such a man provides a stable center of a world of illusion and flux. He is allied to the spirit, lives in the moment and radiates its serenity to all walks of life. In his book *Emerson's Angle of Vision: Man and Nature in the American Experience* (1952), Sherman Paul comments:

> In the desire to become a Spheral man, to touch the universe on all sides, to merge with it and transfer it to himself, correspondence provided the way to all experience. Even if one confronted the universe only in the limited arc of individual experience, still the faith in the doctrine of leasts—in representative parts and representative levels or degrees guaranteed its circularity and universality. Read correspondentially, history, too aggrandized the self... everything the past of books and the present of nature, could be assimilated by the self; for the self becomes spheral in what George Herbert Mead has called "the reflective mood of self awareness" in what we have already seen as the projection of the self in forms of nature only by objectifying itself was the self knowable, and only by taking up all the world as itself was its sphericity attained.[13]

Thus the force of character is cumulative.

Having underlined the primacy of 'self-trust' in man (the Transcendental man), Emerson delves into the reasons behind self-trust. Who is the trustee? What is the "aboriginal self" on which a universal reliance may be placed? This led to the essence of genius, virtue, and life, to the primary wisdom or intuition. Man's intuitive powers stem from his being part of the first cause, his divine nature: "We first share the life by which things exist and afterwards see them as appearances in nature and forget that we have shared their cause."[14] Thus, the perceptions of the soul cannot be interpreted in terms of philosophy. Nor does the soul require a human intermediary or a "prop" in its relation to the Divine Spirit.

The *summum bonum* of Emerson's theory of the Transcendental man, as also his belief in self-reliance is that the soul masters man because it works and "is"—"who has more obedience than I masters me, though he should not raise his finger. Round him I must revolve by the gravitation of Spirits."[15] A further attribute of being self-reliant or soul- reliant is that it helps unify the duality in man and bring together the mystic and the practical in man. This is because the soul depends upon the Divine, the "ever-blessed one" whose attributes permeate down to all aspects of life vis-à-vis commerce, husbandry, hunting, whaling, etc.

In being self-reliant, man imitates nature:

> Nature suffers nothing to remain in her Kingdom which cannot help itself. The genesis and maturation of a planet, its poise and orbit, the bended recovering itself from the strong wind, the vital resources of every animal and vegetable are demonstrations of the self-sufficing and therefore self-relying soul.[16]

Placing the "self" at the centre of the transcendental view of man, self-reliance becomes synonymous with God-reliance. Thus, the self-reliant or transcendental man does not indulge in any sort of antinomianism, which is characteristic of the material or animal man. He relies upon the highest intuitions from the inner voice. This leads to a unique relation between man and nature.

When a person is self-reliant or God-reliant, the natural world becomes a paradise since (by postulate) the phenomenal world is at best "a remoter incarnation of Deity" and dependent upon man's spiritual condition for its "effects." In his 'historical' introduction to Transcendentalism, Kenneth Walter Cameron emphasizes the fact that Nature was a kind of mediator between the "Over-Soul" and mankind: "It takes the place of Torah in Jewish theology."[17] The rich "ministry" of Nature to man is seen both in the Coleridgean and Sweden-borgian systems." Emerson sums them up in his little book, *Nature* (1836).

Nature arose out of what Emerson called a "Saturnalia" of faith; in the last three chapters, it becomes a paean to the mighty "self" which governs the objective universe. The same ecstasy informs the two seminal addresses: "The American Scholar" and "The Divinity School Address."

On August 11, 1841, Emerson delivered a lecture entitled 'The Method of Nature' before the society of the Adelphi in the Water Ville College, Maine. In his address, he affirmed that nature was a living testimony to man, a witness to his days and ways:

> In the divine order, intellect is primary, nature secondary; it is the memory of the mind that which once existed in intellect as pure Law, has now taken body as nature....We can never be quite strangers or inferiors in nature. It is flesh of our flesh, and bone of our bone. But we no longer hold it by the hand; we have lost our miraculous power, our arm is no more as strong as the frost, nor our will equivalent to gravity and the elective attractions. Yet we can use nature as a convenient standard, and the meter of our rise and fall. It has this advantage as a witness, it cannot be debauched. When man curses, nature still testifies to truth and love. We may therefore safely study the mind in nature because we cannot steadily gaze on it in mind, as we explore the face of the sun in a pool, when our eyes cannot brook his direct splendour.[18]

The relationship between man and nature is complex. On the one hand, nature is a "Witness" to man. On the other, man provides the key to nature. Since man is a microcosm, he is also the veritable key to all existence—the cosmos. Both Coleridge and Emerson believed that the best analysis of the material universe was through the mind. And since matter and mind "coincided," the one unlocking the other and both penetrated by the same "Divine unity," then the great ideas of the mind of man were paralleled by the great unifying "Laws" organising the Kingdom of Nature.

Coleridge believed in the great 'Law of Polarity', which not only manifested itself in Physics by positive and negative poles of the magnet, in Botany and Zoology by male and female sexes, but throughout existence by the antithesis of mind and matter. Nature's 'ministry' to man, according to Coleridge's system, can be summed up in the following words:

> Be great, O man, since God hath so richly blessed thee! Trust thy Higher Self! Yea, Know thyself! awake thy sleeping Reason! let thy will subjugate the sense—loving understanding ! so shalt thou know God and partake of his Divine Being, for knowing is becoming, and the reverse is equally true. "Quantum Sumus, Seimus!" the more spiritual thou becomes— the more of spirit shalt thou see in the world. Everything is a microcosm for which God is the infinite solution.[19]

Emerson, on his part, likewise analysed Nature. He saw Nature as (a) Practical use of Commodity; (b) Beauty; (c) Symbolic language; (d) Spiritual discipline; (e) Revelation of the Spirit or Over-Soul in mystical moments. Thus, Nature 'ministers' to man. It is essential for the moral and physical well-being of man:

> There is the bucket of cold water from the spring, the wood fire to which the chilled traveller rushes for safety—and there is the sublime moral of autumn and of noon. We nestle in nature, and draw our living and prerequisites from her roots and grains, and we receive glances from the heavenly bodies, which call us to solitude and foretell the remotest future...[20]

Nature has two aspects: *Natura Naturata* or visible nature, which delights with its abundant beauty, 'beauty breaks in everywhere' and *Natura Naturans* or the Secret working of Nature, the quick cause before which all forms 'flee as driven snows.' It is the *Natura Naturans* which makes for evolution, for the flora and fauna, the trilobites, quadruped and man. "It is a long way from granite to the oyster, farther yet to Plato and the preaching of immortality of the soul. Yet all must come, as surely as the first atom has two sides."[21] Thus, man, because of his spiritual affinities, may enter Nature at the physical level and step by step in a mystical initiation realise his identity with the cosmic spirit.

'Wood notes' printed in *The Dial* in two instalments (Oct. 1840 and Oct. 1841) explores the process of initiation. In the four sections of the poem, we see the successive masks of personae: the poet, the forest seer, and the peasant. They are symbolic figures showing man's increasing involvement with Nature. The first personae—the poet has abandoned society, while the culminating figure—the peasant represents man under the unceasing sway of Nature.

The poet "Caesar of his leafy Rome" having left his society behind, enters the "Woodland Walks." He approaches Nature with a receptive child-like submission, having laid aside all hostility—the fishing rod, gun or scythe. He is alive to feelings of wonder, love, enchantment and knowledge. The initiation begins with a tentative feeling, a mood "sure some God his eye enchants." Enchantment gives way to knowledge. A knowledge-based upon the Romantic Intuition as against Lockean Empiricism.

The poet is entranced by the profusion of the phenomenal world—shadows, colours, clouds, grass-buds, caterpillar shrouds and the like. He also wonders at the laws governing Nature: "Why Nature loves the number five and why the star forms—she repeats."[22]

The sense of enchantment, wonder and knowledge leads the poet to an all embracing cosmic love: "lover of all things alive." Love in turn leads the poet to the greatest mystery. Having penetrated the heart of nature, he is left with the enigma of the "Self":

> Wonderer at all he meets
> Wonderer chiefly at himself
> Who can tell him what he is
> or how meet in human elf
> coming and past eternities.[23]

Thus, the poet goes into nature to discover his identity, which, as the poem develops is co-extensive with the universe.

In section two, the 'forest-seer' takes us into the secret hiding places of nature. His initiation is a product of intuition. He lays bare the magic of Nature. "It seemed as if the breezes brought him/It seemed as if the sparrows taught him."[24]

The phenomenal world, *i.e. Nature Naturata* in a state of magical sympathy yields its secrets. However, the forest seer is aided at another level by his own "secret 'sight' which makes him realise" where, in far fields, the orchids grew, "Having partaken of the 'Natura Naturan's,' the great inhering principle of nature which yields to this "lover true". He enters in a secret intimacy with nature and penetrates her inner most recesses, "And the shy hawk did wait for him."

Section three of the poem deals with how man's spiritual shortcomings are exposed in contact with primeval nature. In the wildest nature of "unploughed Maine", the "lumberer's gang" represents the materialistic and destructive purposes of man as "the aged pine-tree fall" under the axe and the Lumberers are to be regarded, therefore, as the savage excess (Aristotelian distinction of the mean, the excess, and the defect).

Section four shows us the culminating figure of "the musing peasant, lowly great". The initiation reaches its climax with the human being "at the heart of the scene." Unlike the forest seer who pursues nature, the peasant is at home with nature "the public child of earth and sky." The tenor of the poem is Wordsworthian—"for nature ever faithful is, to such as trust her faithfulness."[25]

There is yet again a re-affirmation of magical sympathy which yields 'like-to-like.' The concluding passage on death is appropriate. Death is the liberation of man. It will return him to nature from whence he began. Nature will yield "A pillow in her greenest field" for the "departed lover" of all nature.

While "Wood notes" represents man's ascension in nature, Emerson was alive to the possibility of man's descent. Carl F. Strauch, in his essay, "Emerson and the Doctrine of Sympathy" comments: "for the present generation of students Emerson's handling of the doctrine may be more fascinating as we descend on the scale. Man increasingly seeks out the physical or materialistic in nature to this excess in his own make-up."[26]

This theme is explored in his poem "Guy." Guy is shrewd and witty and has "caught nature in his snares." Perhaps a modern-day equivalent would be Gerald Crich in D.H. Lawrence's *Women in Love,* also used nature to serve his materialistic ends. The poem functions at two levels. On the surface, it appears that both, at the spiritual and physical levels, there is a "secret" to mastering life. The poem appears to celebrate the materialistic exploiter of that 'secret.' But at another level, there is total rejection. The poem is divided into two equal parts by the couplet. "It seemed his genius discreet/Worked on the Maker's own receipt."[27]

The first part of the poem delineates the qualities inherent in man— "mortal mixed of middle clay/attempered to the night and day."[28] Guy, in keeping with the Neo-platonic scale, stands at the midway point, a little above the average human being. He has intimations of cosmic sympathy and power. "Guy possessed the talisman/that all things from him began."[29]

Guy has, in a sympathetic rapport, mastered life. He is invulnerable, in possession of occult power, which is seen in his exploitative success with "obedient Nature." Thus, no element of nature can harm him, "aimed at him, the blushing blade/ Healed as fast the wounds it made."[30]

He is equipped with formidable powers, "If on the faeman fell his gaze/Him it would straight way blind or craze."[31] Thus, Guy turns nature to his advantage. Even disaster helps rather than hinders him. "There was no frost but welcome came/Nor fresh et, nor midsummer flame."[32] Nature vainly attempts to escape his "snares." "Steam could not so perversely wind/But corn of Guy's was there to grind."[33]

Guy bends nature to his materialistic ends. "Belonged to wind and world the toil/And venture, and to Guy the oil."[34]

Nature operates on the principle of 'Like-to-like,' at whatever level man chooses. Guy's level is that of materialistic gain, physical power, and occult magic. Nature responds likewise. Guy is "interchangeable with things," he is essentially and ultimately only a 'thing' himself. Thus, the last laugh is on Guy. There is however, the possibility of a descent below and beyond the materialistic attraction between man and nature.

In "Himatreya", Emerson explores the horror of absolute universal nothingness, thereby anticipating by "a good many years E.M. Forster's ugly "boun" in *A Passage to India.*"[35] "Himatreya" is Emerson's most sharply accentuated commentary on the physical sympathies between man and nature on the scale downward to extinction. The poem has three speakers, two of them paired in the fatal connection of like-to-like. The first is the Yankee Landlord, materialistic and earth-bound, and the second is Earth, a sub-divinity—darkly primitive and universal. The poem functions on a pattern of ironies. When the landlord says that his property knows him, as does his dog, he is relating to the land, and when he further adds, "We sympathise," he is unwittingly preparing for the inexorable truth that in keeping with the doctrine of like-to- like, death "adds him to his land, a lump of mould the more."

Having dealt at length upon the primacy of the 'Self' and 'Nature' to the Transcendental man, we come to the question of the Transcendental outlook upon ultimate reality that is to the third factor in the triangle of Man, Nature and the Over- Soul. Man and Nature have value only to the extent the Transcendent Spirit shines in them. The Over-Soul is both above man's comprehension and also 'within' him as an 'incarnate Logos.' Thus, the true self in man is the "Transcendent Self." In his essay "Transcendentalism and Emerson," Howard Mumford Jones comments: "Emerson even goes so far as to imply that God and man or at least man in his highest potentiality, are virtually one."[36]

This would explain the fact that the Transcendental man is basically the divine man. In his essay "The Over-Soul", Emerson affirms, "Ineffable is the union of man and God in every act of the soul. The simplest man who in his integrity worships God becomes God."[37] The immense possibilities and potentialities in man solved the problem of evil, or rather, reduced it to nothing. In his essay "Compensation", Emerson argues that the Soul "is" the only constant factor in the ebb and flow of life:

> God is not a relation or a part, but the whole. Being is the vast affirmative, excluding Negation self balanced....

> Vice is the absence or departure of the same....Falsehood, may indeed stand as the great night or shade on which as a background the living universe paints itself forth, but no fact is begotten by it, it cannot work, for it is not. It cannot work any good, it cannot work any harm.[38]

Thus, Emerson remained untouched, even oblivious to the problem of evil, and that "stain upon the soul", which was to preoccupy writers like Nathaniel Hawthorne and Herman Melville, leading to their tragic vision of man.

Having delved into the triangular relationship between Man, Nature and the Over-Soul, what remains to be stated is that the central thrust of Emerson's exploration of man is his assumption that whatever truth lay beyond or outside man, can only be reached through and by him. Emerson's life and letters read like an invocation to the Transcendental man, "I stand here to say, let us worship the mighty and Transcendent Soul,"[39] whose advent he never doubted even for a moment and goes on to affirm: "It is the office, I doubt not, of this age to annul that adulterous divorce which the superstition of many ages affected between intellect and holiness."40 Having overcome the hiatus between Man and God, Emerson was able to unite them forever in the person of the "Transcendental Man."

End Notes

1. William Ellery Channing, "Unitarian Christianity," Sermon at the ordination of Rev. Jared Sparks in Baltimore.
2. *Ibid.*
3. Perry Miller, ed., *The American Transcendentalists: Their Prose and Poetry* (Garden City: Doubleday Anchor Books, 1957).
4. Ralph Waldo Emerson, "Illusions".
5. Kenneth Walter Cameron, *Young Emerson's Transcendental Vision: An Exposition of his World View with an Analysis of the Structure, Background and Meaning of Nature* (1836) (Hartford: Transcendental Books, 1971), 7-15.
6. *Ibid.*, 7-15.
7. Jeffrey L. Duncan, *The Power and Form of Emerson's Thought* (Charlottesville: University Press of Virginia, 1973), 44-56.

8. Ralph Waldo Emerson, *Essays: First and Second Series* (New Delhi: Eurasia Publishing House, 1965), 31.
9. *Ibid.*, 32.
10. *Ibid.*, 31.
11. *Ibid.*, 32.
12. *Ibid.*, 34.
13. Sherman Paul, *Emerson's Angle of Vision: Man and Nature in American Experience* (Cambridge: Harvard University Press, 1932), 132-69.
14. Ralph Waldo Emerson, *Essays: First and Second Series* (New Delhi: Eurasia Publishing House, 1965), 37.
15. *Ibid.*, 40.
16. *Ibid.*, 41.
17. Kenneth Walter Cameron, *Young Emerson's Transcendental Vision: An Exposition of his World View with an Analysis of the Structure, Background and Meaning of Nature* (1836) (Hartford: Transcendental Books, 1971), 191-223.
18. Perry Miller, ed., *The American Transcendentalists: Their Prose and Poetry* (Garden City: Doubleday Anchor Books, 1957).
19. Kenneth Walter Cameron, *Young Emerson's Transcendental Vision: An Exposition of his World View with an Analysis of the Structure, Background and Meaning of Nature* (1836) (Hartford: Transcendental Books, 1971), 191-223.
20. Ralph Waldo Emerson, *Essays: First and Second Series* (New Delhi: Eurasia Publishing House, 1965) 328.
21. *Ibid.*, "Nature", 332-34.
22. Robert E. Burkholder and Joel Myerson, ed., *Critical Essays on Ralph Waldo Emerson* (Boston: G.K. Hall & Co., 1983), 326-45.
23. 'Wood notes' *The Dial* 1840-41.
24. *Ibid.*
25. *Ibid.*
26. Carl F. Strauch, "Emerson and the Doctrine of Sympathy: Studies in Romanticism," 6 (Spring, 1967), 152-74.
27. "Guy".
28. *Ibid.*
29. *Ibid.*
30. *Ibid.*
31. *Ibid.*

32. *Ibid.*
33. *Ibid.*
34. *Ibid.*
35. Carl F. Strauch, "Emerson and the Doctrine of Sympathy: Studies in Romanticism", 6 (Spring, 1967), 152-74.
36. Howard Mumford Jones, "Transcendentalism and Emerson." *Interpretations: Essays on American Literature*, ed., R.K. Gupta (Hyderabad: ASRC, 1967), 48-69.
37. "The Over-Soul", 173.
38. "Compensation", 71.
39. "The Method of Nature."
40. *Ibid.*

2

Thoreau: At Home With Nature

There is a flower known to botanists, one of the same genus with our summer plant called "Life- Everlasting," a Gnaphalium like that, which grows on the most inaccessible cliffs of the Tyrolese mountains, where the chamois dare hardly venture, and which the hunter, tempted by its beauty, and his love (for it is immensely valued by the Swiss maidens), climbs the cliffs to gather, and is sometimes found dead at the foot, with the flower in his hand. It is called by botanists the Gnaphalium leontopodium, but by the Swiss 'Edelweisse', which signifies Noble Purity. Thoreau seemed to me living in the hope to gather this plant, which belonged to him by right.

"Thoreau"[1]

—Ralph Waldo Emerson

Henry David Thoreau, Concord born and bred, of a rebellious and reflective nature, and a close associate of Emerson, presents an enigmatic figure. Attempts to classify him prove not only varied but frustrating. Charles Frederick Briggs qualifies Thoreau as a Yankee Diogenes and Emerson says that Thoreau "...was bred to no profession, he never married; he lived alone; he never went to church; he never voted; he refused to pay a tax to the state; he ate no flesh; he drank no wine; he never knew the use of tobacco; and, though a naturalist, he used neither trap nor gun."[2]

To his poet friend and biographer Ellery Channing, Thoreau was the poet-naturalist, a lover of woodland beauty. To the abolitionist Franklin Sanborne, he was a Concord warrior. Lowell saw him as a 'gone to seed' transcendentalist. To Stevenson, full of Victorian Vigor, Thoreau was a simple skulker.

Thoreau fared little better in the twentieth century. Paul Elmer More saw him as one of Rousseau's wild men moving towards the self-restraint of Neo-Humanism. John Macy, the socialist critic, considered him a powerful literary radical. Lewis Mumford linked him to the National and State parks. His French biographer Leon Bazalgette saw him as a savage, one of Chateaubriand's noble red men in the Virgin forest. Parrington links Thoreau to economics and considers Walden a handbook to refute Adam Smith. To Constantine Rourke, he appears a "Slick" Yankee peddler, and to Gilbert Zeldes, he is an antinomian.

Thoreau certainly appears to be an ambiguous character. Ludwig Lewisohn, an amateur sexologist, felt that Thoreau was hopelessly inhibited to the point of physical impotence. Van Wyck Brooks sees him as a charming New England eccentric. Edward Dahlberg goes so far as to claim that Thoreau was a philosophic anarchist and an earlier Lawrence. To sum it all, he appears to Henry Seidel Canby as a neurotic, sublimating his passions through a loving study of Nature. Be it as it may, the hall- mark of Thoreauvian thought appears to be a venture into Nature, an interest initiated by his mentor Ralph Waldo Emerson. Thoreau imbibed the basic tenets of Transcendentalism and was deeply influenced by Emerson's *Nature*. In order to understand the crux of Thoreauvian thought, his assumption of man as a romantic naturalist, one has to keep in mind the formative influence of Emerson on Thoreau, especially between his graduation from Harvard and his move to the Woods by Walden Pond. The importance of Nature was all too apparent to Emerson. Man was a "God in ruins," only dimly in touch with the divine sources within him, and the natural world remained "the...expositor of the divine."[3] It is up to man, now degenerate but endowed with divine gifts to read that exposition so readily available in Nature. Another important aspect of Emerson's rediscovery of Nature was that a man's excursions into nature become a means of recovering his own "power," his charismatic capacity for the mastery of life. Thoreau was to make use of a like principle to resurrect his inner life at Maiden pond. Further, it was Emerson's enunciation of the principle of "correspondence" which helped Thoreau realise how the pattern of renewal works in the actual experience of Nature. In "Language", Emerson asserts "particular Natural facts are symbols of particular Spiritual facts."[4] As a man studies the details of Nature, he discovers the natural and spiritual law that operates within him. *Walden* is replete with instances of "correspondence" between man and Nature. Thoreau was comprehensive in his quest for Nature. Not only are the virtues in man represented in Nature, but it also mirrors his vices. When Thoreau saw the ugly or sensual in Nature, he analysed it as a symbol of ugliness or sensuality in himself. Correspondence seems a perfect means for ensuring one's relation to Nature. All facts, even unpleasant ones, are part of the grand quest of the self. Thus, to a great extent, Thoreauvian thought seems grounded in Emersonian transcendentalism. However, beyond a point, Thoreau takes off on the highway of romantic Naturalism, leaving Emerson's brand of transcendentalism behind.

Thoreau was aware of an innate contradiction in Emerson's *Nature*. On the one hand, Emerson asserted that Nature should be studied by living in it, in order to understand God's revelation secretly imprinted upon it. On the other hand, Emerson felt that Nature was insignificant in itself, even untrustworthy. In the first edition of *Nature,* Emerson quotes Plotinus "Nature is but an image or imitation of wisdom, the last thing of the soul, nature being a thing which doth only do, but not know."[5] Thus, Emerson urges man not merely to return to Nature but also urges him to bring Nature under the sway of man's Spirit, so that the universe may become entirely Spiritual. Man uses Nature only to rise above it to the Spiritual life; thus, Nature is subordinate to the divine man:

> The Kingdom of man over Nature, which Cometh not with observation—a dominion such as now is beyond his dream of God—he shall enter without more wonder than the blind man feels who is gradually restored to perfect sight.[6]

Nature has no intrinsic value; it exists as the symbol of Spirit. Emerson argues in "Spiritual Laws" that "Not in Nature but in man" is all the beauty and worth he sees. The world is empty and is indebted to his gilded, exalted soul for all its pride 'earth fills her lap with splendors' not her own. However, unlike Emerson, Thoreau was not interested in building "a Kingdom of man over Nature." He sought a partnership of equals with it. He thought of Nature as a foster mother to a poetic child. His method lay in going to the woods, forgetting the conscious self, and letting Nature be. Thus, Nature has a divinity to which he appeals. He was more interested in the landscape than Emerson, as also in the wild Nature in himself and other men. He wanted to get out of his mind and live in his natural body—which in Emerson's definition, was a mere feature of the 'Not-Me.' Distinct from Emerson, Thoreau gave full expression to Nature's sensuous life and made room for its mystery. Thoreau adopts a working compromise between Spirit and Nature in himself. According to this compromise, man needs Nature to renew himself, to recover his natural healthy life, but Nature also needs and fosters man as her highest creation and representative. Man as the poet personae celebrates or "publishes" the truth of Nature, he does not distrust or deny it. Nature is, for him, a powerful and mysterious independent realm, not a mere projection of himself. But Nature is inarticulate, it is useless to man unless he perceives and describes it. This is Thoreau's version of Emersonian Idealism. Thoreau laid stress on inspired and creative human perception. A man must educate his senses so that man may contribute to his regeneration. The perception of Thoreau was not only visual and spiritual, but also sensuous and natural. He sought a more natural and unconscious way of being. The desire to naturalize himself exists alongside his desire for the spiritual: "I found in myself, and still find, an instinct towards a higher, or, as it is named, spiritual life, as do most men, and another towards a primitive rank and savage one, and I reverence them both. I love the wild not less than the Good" (Walden, 210).

Thus, in spite of the fact that the genesis of Thoreauvian thought can be traced to Emersonian Transcendentalism, it is as a romantic Naturalist that Thoreau breaks new ground. Perry

Miller, in one of his last essays, places Thoreau in "The context of international romanticism."[7] Miller felt that Thoreau struggled throughout his career with the traditional romantic problems of "balance" and "combination" with the world outside. As a romantic naturalist, Thoreau felt that man should dwell close to the channels in which his life flowed, to be in perfect correspondence with Nature, to be "at home with Nature." However, this is easier said than done. A romantic is no longer related to the Social and Cosmic order by codified inherited ties; he is a man alone with his imagination. This isolation adds to his creative life, his desire to forge an "original relation with the universe." Emerson, Thoreau, Melville, Hawthorne, Whitman and Poe, in keeping with the American sensibility of their time, felt their connection with the greater European past frayed or severed. As "isolators" they had to construct their imaginative lives. Thoreau chose to fashion his in Nature. However, his concept of Nature was romantic. He saw Nature as one, alive and the aggregate of all things. His concept is identical to Réne Wellek's romantic formula for Nature "as a living whole." Réne Wellek saw Nature as "a living, growing, organic entity infused with Spirit and in some way related to man."[8] The concept of "Nature as a living whole" though appropriated by the romantics, is not of romantic origin. It is an ancient belief in keeping with the human desire for an erotic relation with the land. It was part of the Hellenistic world and was part and parcel of such cults as Orphism. In the Christian era, this concept surfaced subversively, even heretically. In the eighteenth and nineteenth centuries, it appealed to romantic writers with renewed power.

In keeping with the romantic heritage, Thoreau shared alike a romantic dilemma. All Romantics are aware of this separation from Nature, however, they desire to be at home with it. Thus, the romantic poet finds his chief problem in his consciousness of isolation and separation. A major effort of romantics like Thoreau is to come to terms with the separation from Nature. Thoreau, like Wordsworth and Goethe, fought intimation that Nature was estranged and alien to him. Yet such doubts did occur and Thoreau gave them a place in his works.

Thoreau's major weapon against the estrangement with Nature was his belief in Emerson's idea of correspondence, according to which Nature and mind are thought to have essentially identical structures. However, it is not always possible to identify with Nature spontaneously, in such instances, correspondence becomes a conception imposed by the mind on Nature. Thus, the romantic is forced to adhere to Schelling's "Nature Philosophie", who espoused nature not only because man needed it but also felt that man must choose to establish a relation with it:

> So long as I am identified with Nature, I understand what a living Nature is as well as I understand my own life; I realise how this general life of Nature reveals itself in the most various forms, in step-by-step development, in gradual approaches to freedom. But as soon as I separate myself (and with me the whole ideal realm) from nature, nothing remains for me but a dead object and I cease to understand how life outside me is possible.[9]

Schelling makes it clear that relation with nature is not automatic. The romantic has a choice, either to see Nature as bearing with affinity to man or see it without affinity. A man's realisation of Nature becomes an act of Will and of awareness. In the *Week*, Thoreau makes it clear that his romantic faith is a conscious discovery: "...As if our birth had first sundered things, and we had been thrust up through Nature like a Wedge, and not till the wound heals and the scar disappears do we begin to discover where we are, and that Nature is one and continuous everywhere" (W, I, 372). Thoreau tried to maintain his sense of Nature as one and continuous and identical to man. However, there are moments when he does not find his cherished affinity, when Nature becomes for him a dead object, or even an object of terror. The fear of Nature turning into a vacuum is all too real. Herman Melville was to objectify this threat in his great allegorical work *Moby-Dick*. Thoreau was forever making Schelling's choice to believe, but he would often vacillate in this choice.

Thoreau was a romantic in his basic attitude towards Nature. Further, he was a romantic Naturalist like Wordsworth or Goethe who gave Nature the dignity of an independent status. Thus, he differed from Blake, Shelley and Fitche, the anti-naturalists who regard Nature at best as material to be transformed by the human mind and imagination or at worst as a seductive and dangerous power in the self and the world which "must be overcome." The romantic, who is an anti-naturalist, either ignores the landscape or loves it warily. The romantic naturalist, on the other hand, feels that a total possession of Nature by the separated mind leads to a selfish and dangerous distortion of the observed world, a way of killing the God they need. Thus a romantic naturalist conceives of the imagination as reconciled to Nature, not controlling it or wholly transforming it; there is an imaginative balance behind mind and Nature. Thoreau, on his part, seems to go to extremities with regard to mind and Nature. Sometimes, he experimented with self-forgetfulness and dissolved all cultural, civilized, mental patterns choosing to submerge himself in unconscious sympathy with the chaos of Nature, giving little mental shape to the Cosmos. On the other hand, Thoreau was drawn to the mind's party, which seemed too apparent every now and then. Thoreau was aware of this when he looked on the Atlantic from Cape Cod. Northrop Frye comments: "The (romantic) Landscape is a veil dropped over the naked nature of screaming rabbits and gasping stags, the nature red in tooth and claw which haunted a later generation."[10]

Consistent with his fear of violence in the eternal world is the romantic's fear of nature within him, which makes him painfully or joyfully aware of his aggressiveness. Thoreau, in some of his excursions sets forth in high animal spirits to confront the wilderness but then comes to the awareness that his adventurousness is an illusion and that his wilderness must be chastened. Finally, there comes a stage when for some romantics all correspondence breaks down when Nature is not considered in terms of life and growth and it appears as mere power or chaos. In "Ktaadn," Thoreau felt himself violently and suddenly ready to qualify Coleridge's "Dejection."

"O Lady! we receive but what we give, and in our life alone does Nature live."[11] Thoreau had an ambiguous attitude towards Nature. On occasions he was even distrustful of Nature as is recorded in his journal of 1834:

> We soon get through with Nature. She excites an expectation which she cannot satisfy. The merest child which has rambled into a copsewood dreams of a Wildness so wild and strange and inexhaustible as Nature can never show him... (J, VI, 293)

Another question which beset Thoreau in his advent into Nature was to what extent could a romantic naturalist participate in Nature. As a romantic, he could participate in the cyclical pattern of Nature's growth, death, decay and rebirth, but as an intellectual he was wary of its malevolent aspects. The poet feels cut off from nature. This is what Thoreau felt as he watched the Mt. Katahdin rocks. At such a moment, she abandons his effort to include all nature in his vision and prefers to restrict his affection for nature to its kindest aspects.

In spite of the apparent difficulties of being "at home with nature", Thoreau along with the other great romantic naturalists like Goethe and Wordsworth persists in his efforts to revive the ancient belief in nature. Further, the romantic naturalists tried to posit the belief that a relation between a nineteenth-century 'isolate', and Nature was not only necessary but possible. All the romantics participate in the effort to put the isolated self and the "Not-Me" back together again. In Coleridge's letter to William Sotheby he writes "We are all one life. A poet heart and intellect should be combined, intimately combined and unified with the great appearances of Nature."[12]

A romantic believes that a man becomes creative when he can assert his relation to the whole to which he belongs, when he can stimulate the intercourse between mind and world, soul and body, subject and object, value and fact, when he sees the minute particulars of existence under the light of the mind's eternity.

Having delved into some of the concerns of the Romantic naturalist, it would be well to see how Thoreau developed his unique vision of man "at home with nature." The fledging Thoreau of the journals as essays written after his graduation from Harvard (1837) and before the experiment at Walden Pond (1845), is not very consistent in his approaches to Nature. James McIntosh underlines three different modes of dealing with nature in the early Thoreau. "The mode of involvement (a willful sharing of the wild nature); the mode of detachment (an aware contemplation of a separate nature); and the mode of comprehensive understanding (an attempt to know and feel nature as a whole)."[13]

The first mode gave rise to a sensitivity to the pulsating vibrant hues of Nature: "men tire me when I am not constantly greeted and refreshed by the flux of sparkling streams. Surely joy is the condition of life. Think of the young fry that leap in ponds, the myriads of insects ushered into being on a summer evening..." ("Natural History of Massachusetts", W, V, 106). The emphasis is on all the joyful, earthly here-and-now. He delights in the splendid life he sees teeming around him. In order to become close to nature, Thoreau realised he had to be involved with all aspects of Nature. The romantic naturalist must accept even the disagreeable aspects of nature; swamps, gnats, mosquitoes, the chaotic, the dark and the wild in nature "would it not be a luxury to stand up to one's chin in some retired swamp for a whole summer's day, scenting the sweet- fern and bilberry blows, and lulled by the minstrelsy of gnats and mosquitoes?"... (J, I, 141-142). The stimulation of nature also brings about another aspect of wilderness in man, his enjoyment of destruction and upheaval:

> Every man is a warrior when he aspires. The soldier is the practical idealist; he has no sympathy with matter, he revels in the annihilation of it. So do we all at times. When a freshet destroys the works of man, or a fire consumes them, or a Lisbon earthquake shakes them down, our sympathy with persons is swallowed up in a wider sympathy with the universe. A crash is apt to grate agreeably on our ears. (J, I, 135)

Thus, since a romantic naturalist sympathises with Nature, he also allows for natural violence. Thoreau was aware that he enjoyed the storm without because it corresponded with the storm within. Thus, involvement with nature meant a willful lack of control, a surrender to unconscious or natural forces. The human type that Thoreau celebrates at this time is the soldier, who is caught up in violence. Beyond a point, Thoreau withdraws from the dangers of involvement, at the same time, he desires to preserve a closeness to Nature. He does so by assuming a "poet" personae that is a conscious human capable of detachment as well as involvement. By the term "poet", Thoreau did not mean a maker of verses but a man of inspired genius and imagination, whose specific task is that of romantic combination. The poet or self-conscious imaginative man cannot wholly lose himself in nature. There is a part that stands aside, and is detached, for example, in "The Thaw":

> I saw the civil sun drying earth's tears—Her tears of joy that only faster flowed, Fain would I stretch me by the highway side. To thaw and trickle with the melting snow, That mingled soul and body with the tide, I too may through the pores of nature flow. But I alas nor trickle can nor fume, One jot to forward that great work of time, 'Tis mine to hearten while these ply the loom, So shall my silence with their music chime. (Collected Poems, 107)

The poet alone contemplates in a detached manner the work he contemplates. Thus, the attitude of early Thoreau to Nature is to stand back from nature in an attitude of affection and reverence. In his reverence, he contributes both to the harmony of Nature and ennobles himself. The poet is seen as being equal but separate from nature:

> He must be something more than natural,—even super natural. Nature will not speak through but along with him. His voice will not proceed from her midst but, breathing on her, will make her the expression of his thought. He then poetizes when he takes a fact out of nature into Spirit. He speaks without reference to time or place. His though is one world, hers another. Kindly offices do they perform for one another. Each publishes the other's truth. (J, I, 74-75)

The early Thoreauvian attitude towards nature is ambiguous. He seemed to use nature both to get deeply involved with it and to get beyond it. He desires to be both a savage whose eyes revolve in a "Slime" of health and aspires toward "a Wilderness so wild and strange and inexhaustible as Nature can never show him."[14] Both these desires find their way into his great masterpieces, the *Week* and *Walden*, which are just so many attempts to naturalise man, place him in the heart of Nature.

A Week on the Concord and Merrimack Rivers seems at first glance, a baffling book, a compendium of sentiments and memories gathered together during the 1840s on a voyage to Plum Island and Concord. The river is accurately presented: "The sluggish artery of the Concord meadows steals thus unobserved through the town, without a murmur or a pulse- beat, its general course from South-West to North-East, and its length about fifty miles..." (W, I, 9-10). Apart from its physicality, it has another dimension as Thoreau and his brother John very well realize "We seemed to be embarked on the placid current of our dreams, floating from past to future as silently as one awakes to fresh morning or evening thoughts." (W, I, 17). Another interesting aspect of the *Week* is that there is a tendency in Thoreau to make the gap between man and Nature as wide as possible and then bridge it forcefully together. Thus, Thoreau is still at work with the romantic combination to yoke opposites together. This is amply clear in the rubric Thoreau uses to introduce the Week:

> I am bound, I am bound, for a distant shore. By a lonely isle, by a far Azore. There it is, there it is, the treasures I seek, On the barren sands of a desolate creek. (W, I, 2)

On the one hand, Thoreau enjoys the pleasures of a local scene, and on the other, he dreams of the far-off Azores.

The desire that dominates the first two chapters of the *Week* is that of involvement. A desire to make good the Maxim "Surely joy is the condition of life." Thoreau expresses his desire for wildness, his lust for the creative tumult. Thus, his narrative begins in this mood of sensual expectancy towards Nature. Nature is a hulking goddess, who after "dripping and oozing from every pore" respires "more healthy than ever" (W, I, 12). Thoreau sees Nature as "Phusis", a mythical personification of all that Thoreau felt in the glee and sap of the river scene. The brothers are aware that they are privy to Nature's developing plan. They leave the quiet village behind in the face of Nature's vast strangeness. As they pitch camp, they are enveloped in Nature's other world: "...it was such a leafy wilderness; a place for fauns and satyrs, and where bats hung all day to the rocks, and at evening flitted over the water, and fireflies husbanded their light under the grass and leaves against the night" (W, I, 38-39).

Although the Week was organised in seven "Days" the structure of the book is not easily discernible; the separate essays from which it is composed appear too disconnected for immediate apprehension. However, things appear in a different light when we keep in mind Thoreau's consciousness of Nature and the triple purpose behind the book.

When Thoreau presented Nature in the Week, he meant to represent the Kosmos of Concord and Merrimack, describing not only its geography, botany, animal biology and history but also its mythology. Thus, the mystery of the changing landscape is presented to us day-by-day. The subject of the Week is the living kosmos. Secondly, Thoreau wanted to write a "natural" book a "hypaethral" or unroofed book, lying open under the other and permeated by it, open to all weathers, not easy to be kept on the shelf" (J, II, 275). In other words, he tried to describe the fecundity, variety and secret unity of nature.

Thoreau's third intention in writing the Week was to reconcile his human imagination with nature doing justice to both. He sought an affectionate balance with nature, an I— Thou relation. Several essays and episodes in the Week are voiced and enacted by a single persona. The persona (Thoreau) acts out a pattern of changing attitude towards nature; from that of a sober observer to a reckless enthusiast and back again. Thoreau begins by being involved in nature, then feels imaginatively limited by it and wants to break free. Finally, he returns to it as solace and discipline. The Week is like "A walk to Wachusett," a journey at two levels: into the circumscribed realm of New England, Nature and into the boundless realm of private thought. In 1839, Thoreau made a voyage to Mt. Washington. In the course of the book, he relates another trip taken in 1844 to saddle Back Mountain in the Berkshires. Both excursions are narratives not only of actual event, but also of symbolic approaches to an ideal realm.

The river on which Thoreau and John find themselves is equally a double symbol. It binds the New England Kosmos together. The brothers imagine themselves not as men of commerce but as "water rats...While, like Sly water-rats, we stole along nearer the shore, looking for a place to pitch our camp" (W, I, 37- 38). At this point, Thoreau would like to think of himself and his brother as involved in nature, blended with the grass and in touch with its secret life. As he listens to the barking of house dogs, he exalts the animal over the human in a desire to be "a dog and bay the moon" (W, I, 40). There is in Thoreau a deep urge to flee the human and institutional and merge with Nature. This leads to his sympathy for the animal—like natural men. Already in "Concord River", he speaks of the River farmers as being greater than Homer or Chaucer or Shakespeare. The natural man, as against the poet, is not a man of imagination and is unconcerned with the affairs of the mind. Thoreau fancies them as giant delvers in the earth, relics of a more natural time. He comes close to them through a process of sympathy and willed negative capability. "I love these sons of earth every mother's son of them, with their great hearts rushing tumultuously in herds from spectacle to spectacle" (W, I, 359). In the Week, Thoreau even eulogises their coarse pleasures, "I love to see the herd of men feeding heartily on coarse and succulent pleasures, as cattle on the husks and stalks of vegetables (W, I, 361). This is a far cry from the spokesman for Noble purity whom we find in Walden. The generosity, fulness, particularity, and mild formlessness of Nature are preferred to the form, limitation, civility and control of art—The Concord farmer to the great poets: "Homer and Shakespeare and Milton and Marvell and Wordsworth are but the rustling of leaves and crackling of twigs in the forest, and there is not yet the sound of any bird. The Muse has never lifted up her voice to sing" (W, I, 328).

Thoreau has a sympathetic understanding of nature. In the Week, the likeness between man and nature is reinforced over and over again in individual images and metaphor; the boat, painted in nature's colours, the cabin roofs reflecting the flight of hawks, the natural men who resemble beasts and trees.

However, the problem that faces the romantic naturalists is that he has needs other than those fulfilled by Nature. The man of imagination is not always the man of nature. Thoreau is conscious at moments, how insufficient nature is for his imaginative demands. His dissatisfaction with nature becomes articulate in a passage from "Tuesday":

> The most stupendous scenery ceases to be sublime when it becomes distinct, or in other words, limited and the imagination is no longer encouraged to exaggerate it. The actual height and breadth of a mountain or a waterfall are always ridiculously small; they are the imagined only that content us, Nature is not made after such a fashion as we would have her. (W, I, 202)

Thoreau's problem in relating the poet in himself to nature is that despite his romantic naturalist inclination, his imagination is constituted differently from Nature. Nature is regular, repetitive, gradual, constant and predictable. Thoreau's rhythm has moments of demi-divine experience and long stretches of blankness, "Whole weeks and months of my summer life slide away in thin volumes like mist and smoke, till at length some warm morning, perchance, I see a sheet of mist blown down the brook to the swamp, and I float as high above the fields with it" (W, I, 314). In a contest between the life of the imagination and the life of Nature, Nature comes second best:

> Nature doth have her dawn each day,
> But mine are far between;
> Content I cry, for, sooth to say.
> Mine brightest are, I ween
> For when my sun doth deign to rise,
> Though it be her noontide,
> Her fairest field in shadow lies
> Nor can my light abide. (W, I, 302)

The imagination encompasses the brightest dawn, while the moderate continuous success of nature seems limited. As a romantic naturalist, Thoreau is involved in the romantic combination of bringing Nature and the imagination together, however problematic the case may be. The two are interrelated and must go hand in hand. Nature provides no lasting satisfaction unless it can be imaginatively transformed. This, then, is the ideal combination "We need to be earth-born as well as heaven-born." (W, I, 405-406). Nature is, thus, a word for the unbroken continuum between material and spiritual. Nature and imagination furnish the life divine:

> We need pray for no higher heaven than the pure senses can furnish, a purely sensuous life. Our present senses are but the rudiments of what they are destined to become. The ears were made, not for such trivial uses as men are wont to suppose, but hear celestial sounds. The eyes were not made for such grovelling uses as they are now put to a worn out by but to behold the beauty now invisible. May we not see God? Are we to put off and amused in this life, as it were with a mere allegory? Is not Nature rightly read, that of which she is commonly taken to be the symbol merely? (W, I, 408)

James MacIntosh comments, "Thoreau would tie his intimations of the heavenly and eternal freely to this world. Nature is the "here" not only of objects but also divine sensations; the sensations come directly from the experience of objects and there is no separation."[15] Once the romantic naturalist solves the dilemma of the romantic combination, nature is realized through a naturalized imagination and purified senses. Man has to be naturalized. In "Friday", Thoreau enunciates this idea.

"Man nowhere, east or west, lives yet a natural life, round which the vine clings, and which the elm willingly shadows. Man would desecrate it by his touch, and so the beauty of the world remains veiled to him. He needs not only to be spiritualized, but naturalized on the soil of earth." (W, I, 405). The goal—naturalized life presented in the Week requires as a prerequisite of purification of the senses. This, Thoreau explored in Walden, thereby carrying romantic naturalism to its ultimate statement on man. Walden appears to be a watershed in Thoreau's career as a romantic naturalist. It is different from "Ktaadn" (which was an account of his first voyage to the Maine Woods, in 1846) and "The Shipwreck" (accounts of two visits to the cohasset beach in 1849 and 1851), which stress his attempts at regaining his romantic balance. Walden also differs from the last Essays "Walking", "Wild Apples", "The Succession of Forest Trees" and "Autumnal Tints", all published between 1860 and 1862 wherein we find Thoreau fairly well entrenched in Nature. *Walden* comes in for special critical acclaim because not only is it liable to be interpreted at different levels, but it is also a frank documentation of Thoreau's personal myth. R.W.B. Lewis in "One Kind of Adam" says: "The Narrator of Walden is witness to a truly new World which the speaker alone has visited, from which he has just returned, and which he is sure every individual ought to visit at least once — not the visible world around, Walden Pond, but an inner world which the Walden experience allowed him to explore."[16] At first glance, however, *Walden* appears an exercise in simplicity or economy. Stanley Edgar Hyman in "Henry Thoreau in our Time" saw *Walden* as an experiment in ecology. It could also feature on the environmentalist agenda. Walden was the product of Thoreau's mature years. The joyous affirmation of the *Week* is past. Walden was written in the years of "decay" when the poetic muse is spent or at least difficult to summon. The Thoreau of this period was looking to Nature for renewal and inspiration and recovery of the lost self. Thoreau sought to build an organic life as consciously as he built his hut. "The grand necessity, then, for our bodies, is to keep warm, to keep the vital heat in us."[17] Thoreau was aware that when the "aim in life is highest", it called for the greatest disciple. The disciple who is finding a "natural center" requires purity, "chastity is perpetual acquaintance with the All." By shunning society, abjuring comfort, by embracing economy, Thoreau was seeking to purify himself and recover the "lost child" he was. The *Walden* chapter was his way of regaining the primal world and a pristine initiation into consciousness. Thoreau was aware that the easiest advent into nature was in the person of a hunter. In his chapter "Higher Laws," Thoreau affirms, "Such is oftenest the young man's introduction to the forest and the most original part of himself. He goes thither at first as a hunter and fisher."[18] Having passed this stage, only does a man approach nature as "a poet or naturalist...and leave the gun and fish-pole behind."[19] Thus, Thoreau substitutes the hunting instinct of the *Week* for the cultivating instruct of the bean field in *Walden*. As mentioned earlier, *Walden* was Thoreau's personal myth, his expression of the micro and macro cosmic relationship. The primitive concern with essentials—building his house, planting, tending, harvesting his beans, fishing were all contributory factors to the process of naturalising. A prerequisite for the exploration of the self: "Direct your eyes inward, and you'll find A thousand regions in your mind yet undiscovered. Travel them, and be Expert in home cosmography."[20]

Walden was Thoreau's quest for the lost self. Purity was the Key to this search. Purity meant a return to the Spring time of life, to the golden age of his youth, when the self was not clouded by self-consciousness.

Walden follows the cycle of developing consciousness, which parallels the change of seasons. A development from the sensuous, external (unconscious, out-of-doors) summer of life through the stages of autumnal consciousness and the withdrawal inward to the self-reflection of Winter, to the ecstatic rebirth in spring. The promised rebirth or regeneration could not be effected without the ritual purification required. The sensual or generative energy which had been dissipated must be controlled and channelised in the proper direction. In "Higher Laws" Thoreau elaborates:

> The generative energy, which, when we are loose, dissipates and makes us unclean, when we are continent invigorates and inspires us. Chastity is the flowering of man; and what are called Genius, Heroism, Holiness, and the like, are but various fruits which succeed it. Man flows at once to God when the channel of purity is open. By turns our purity inspires and our impurity casts us down. He is blessed who is assured that the animal is dying out in him day by day, and the divine being established.[21]

In Walden Pond, Thoreau saw the image of his purified self. The self he sought to recover. As a young man, he had spent many a happy hour at Walden Pond "I have spent many an hour, when I was younger, floating over its surface as the Zephyr willed."[22]

If the Pond Symbolizes his lost self, the "Wood choppers" are no less symbolic of the ravages of time. "My Muse may be excused if she is silent henceforth. How can you expect the birds to sing when their groves are cut down?"[23] The discovery that Thoreau makes at Walden Pond is that although the groves have been cut down, although the self has been ravaged by sensual fires, the true self remains unchanged. Time has laid waste the shores of the pond, the pond itself remains intact. In "The Ponds" Thoreau asserts:

> Why, here is Walden, the same Woodland lake that I discovered so many years ago; where a forest was cut down last winter another is springing up by its shore as lustily as ever, the same thought is welling up to its surface that was then; it is the same liquid joy and happiness to itself and its Maker, ay, and it may be to me....[24]

Thus, the Thoreau-in-decay comes face to face with the undefiled self. The purpose of the *Walden* experiments was to plumb the depths, hit rock bottom, and to discover the truth. Thoreau realizes that the blade of grass—"The green flame of life" is ever present. The process of renewal has taken place. Above all, it brings home to Thoreau the fact that nothing was "inorganic." By sounding the bottom, Thoreau came to an understanding of the Law that governed the universe and helped in his participation of the natural world. He realized that the intersection of the lines of greatest length and breadth coincided with the point of greatest depth. If this were applied to Ethics, then it would imply that "draw lines through the length and breath of the aggregate of man's particular daily behaviour and waves of life into his coves and inlets, and where they intersect will be the height or depth of his character."[25] Thus, it is possible to represent on a graph the moral topography of a person. If this were done of Thoreau, The Pond would be his "eternal center." The building of an organic life was thus a conscious effort. The Wood chopper, the animal man must be educated into consciousness and still retain his innocence. In the total economy of Nature, the once freely taken gift of inspiration must be earned by perceiving the laws of Nature. Thoreau earned his Walden by awaiting the return of spring and by sharing the organic process. All activity then becomes a way of "naturalizing." Thus, he tended his bean field not for food but as an aspect of his sympathy with Nature. It was also an attempt to link the 'Wild' and the 'cultivated.' Above all, it was a descent to the unwarped primal world. "I disturbed the ashes of unchronicled nations who in primeval years lived under these heavens. "[26]

Thoreau realised that in order to delve into the self, one had to dig below the established surface. The prudential value of the bean field experiments came to $16.94 but its spiritual value was that the Massachusetts soil could sustain the seeds of virtue. The seed had not lost its vitality and could spring forth a new generation of men. When Thoreau came to Walden, he built his hut (the container of his vital heat), he used second-hand materials and borrowed tools; thereby showing his dependence on Civilization. He repaid his debt by sharpening the tools by use. Thoreau describes the building of the hut in great detail because, at a symbolic level, at a deeper level, it meant building his body for his soul:

> What of architectural beauty I now see, I know has gradually grown from within outward, out of the necessities and character of the indweller, who is the only builder,—out of some unconscious truthfulness, and nobleness, without ever a thought for the appearance; and whatever additional beauty of this kind is destined to be produced will be preceded by a like unconscious beauty of life.[27]

When Thoreau built his hut, he wanted it to mirror the progressing seasons of developing consciousness, a development which was as organic as the seasons. In Walden, Thoreau's development began in summer, a period when he was in sympathetic communion with Nature. The chapters "Sounds" and "Solitude" reveal the atmospheric presence of Nature so essential to Thoreau. The hut, which he began in spring, was responsive to Nature, of the bodily frame transparent to Nature. He began to inhabit the house when the "north wind had already begun to cool the pond." During Autumn, he "Lathed and plastered" and finally with the approach of winter he built his fireplace and chimney.

By the fireside he lingered communicating with his inner self. In his soul-searching, as he contemplated the pond, he realized that the water though frozen was as sweet as ever, just awaiting the thaw of spring.

The promised rebirth came in spring. Thoreau awoke to a great realization that all of nature corresponded to one idea, one form. The inner vital principle of Nature as of man is one of renewal: "So human life but dies down to its root, and still puts forth its given blade to eternity."[28]

Thus, Thoreau carried romantic naturalism to its ultimate statement on man, which meant the rebirth of the self in the lap of Nature. To be "at home with nature" simply meant living an organic life.

End Notes

1. Emerson, "Thoreau", *Atlantic Monthly* (August, 1862).
2. *Ibid.*
3. E.W. Emerson, ed., *The Complete Works of Ralph Waldo Emerson*, Centenary Edition, 12 Vols. (Boston: Houghton Mifflin, 1903), I, 71, 64-65.
4. Emerson, Works, I, 25.
5. *Ibid.*, 403-404.
6. *Ibid.*, 77.
7. Perry Miller, "Thoreau in the Context of International Romanticism," *New England Quarterly*, 34 (June, 1961), 147-159.
8. Réne Wellek, *Concepts of Criticism* (New Haven: Yale University Press, 1963), 160.
9. F.W.J. Shelling, *Introduction to Ideen Zu einer philosophie der Natur, in Sammtliche Werke*, ed. K.F.A. Shelling (Stuttgart: Cotta, 1855-1861) II, 47-48.
10. Northrop, Frye, ed., *Romanticism Reconsidered* (New York: Columbia University Press, 1963), 21.
11. *The Complete Poetic Works of Samuel Taylor Coleridge*, ed. E.H. Coleridge (Oxford: Clarendon Press, 1957), I, 365.
12. *Collected Letters of Samuel Taylor Coleridge*, ed. Earl Leslie Griggs (Oxford: Clarendon Press, 1956), II, 459.
13. James MacIntosh: *Thoreau as Romantic Naturalist* (ref book, 93).
14. *Ibid.*, 90.

15. *Ibid.*, 173.
16. R.W. B. Lewis, *The American Adam*. Chicago, Illinois, 1955, Lection III of Chapter I, 20-27.
17. Walden, 8, Henry David Thoreau: *Walden and Civil Disobedience*, ed. Owen Thomas, Prentice-Hall of India, New Delhi.
18. *Ibid.*, 141.
19. *Ibid.*, 19. 20. *Ibid.*, 211.
21. *Ibid.*, 146-147.
22. *Ibid.*, 128.
23. Ibid., 128-129.
24. *Ibid.*, 129.
25. *Ibid.*, 192.
26. *Ibid.*, 106.
27. *Ibid.*, 31-32.
28. *Ibid.*, 205.

3

The Problem of Good and Evil in Nathaniel Hawthorne and Herman Melville

> *The heart, the heart,—there was the little yet boundless sphere wherein existed, the original wrong of which the crime and misery of this outward world were mere types. Purify that inward sphere, and the many shapes of evil that haunt the outward, and which now seem almost our only realities, will turn to shadowy phantoms and vanish of their own accord....*
>
> "Earth's Holocaust"
>
> —Nathaniel Hawthorne

Part-I

New England Transcendentalism was ingrained in Emerson. Thoreau, though deeply influenced, preferred to see man in terms of romantic naturalism. Hawthorne kept himself aloof from the transcendental "madness" which gripped New England. Although he had briefly taken part in the Communistic project of Brook farm, he did not share the optimism of the transcendentalists, their passionate certainty in human and American destinies, which were exalted by Emerson in his *Essays,* and Whitman in *Leaves of Grass*. Evil and sin do not touch Emersonian humanity nor threaten Whitman's brotherhood of man which regulates the Cosmos.

Hawthorne, on the other hand, was deeply influenced by the Puritan-soul-searching and the moral implications of sin. His literary accomplishments are inextricably linked with the Puritans. A haunting sense of guilt and the necessity to lay down the burden of inherited Puritan consciousness found Hawthorne returning time and time again to his Puritan roots in his fictional world. Barret Wendell, highlighting this quality in Hawthorne, points out that for Hawthorne, Puritanism was no longer "a way of life but a subject for Literary Art."[1] Thus, in a sense, Hawthorne seems almost a contemporary of Cotton Mather, the greatest of the Puritan Ministers especially remembered for his role in the Salem witch trials and his religious works, *The Wonders of the Invisible World* and *Magnalia Christi Americana* in baroque prose.

Although some critics have looked for the transcendental element in Hawthorne, Stuart Pratt Sherman in *Americans* (1922) called him "a subtle Critic and Satirist of puritanism from the Transcendental point of view," while T.S. Eliot felt "The work of Hawthorne is truly a criticism...of the puritan morality, of the Transcendental morality and the world which Hawthorne knew."[2] However, there were vistas which Hawthorne never visited. Unlike Emerson, Thoreau and Whitman, Hawthorne was no prophet, no reformer, no diver into the God within. His special area of interest laid elsewhere. He was alive to the invisible landscape.

A study of his writings which include *The Scarlet Letter* (1850), *The House of the Seven Gables* (1851), *The Blithedale Romance* (1852), and *The Marble Faun* (1859) would reveal the fact he was working with the inner recesses of the mind and soul. His characters and incidents are just so many symbols of unseen moral Laws. His books turn out to be case histories of men and women afflicted by guilt, by sin, or what he called "a stain upon the Soul."

Hawthorne's fictional characters derive their wealth and beauty from the fact that the writer considers them as consciences in the face of Sin. They are not complete figures nor do they have any previous lives. Their lives begin, as they were, with their guilt or knowledge of guilt and ends with the long-drawn consequences of guilt, moral or otherwise. Thus, Hawthorne delves deeply into his characters, laying bare their very roots. Agostino Lombardo has underlined the fact that Hawthorne offered "psychological portraits" of great characters such as Hester Prynne and the Reverend Dimmesdale in *The Scarlet Letter* or Donatello, Miriam and Hilda in the *Marble Faun*.

Nina Baym, in *The Scarlet Letter: A Reading* (1936), stresses that Hawthorne's novels were concerned with "inner truths" which place his works at the forefront of the development of psychological fiction "in his recognition of the hidden life and his description of mental processes, Hawthorne was a psychologist ahead of his time."[3]

This psychological exploration of man led Hawthorne to wrestle with the problem of good and evil. Hester Prynne, Arthur Dimmesdale, Roger Chillingworth, Judge Pyncheon are just so many attempts at confronting this problem, hence their allegorical and symbolic value. While for Emerson, Thoreau and Whitman, the results of such a quest, delving beneath the surface was always a positive, joyous revelation—a confirmation, whereas for Hawthorne, it was inevitably a revelation of evil: "There is evil in every human heart, which may remain latent, perhaps through the whole of life, but circumstances may rouse it to activity."[4]

There is no escape from the evil that lies in the heart of man. Catholicism offered partial remedies. But absolutions and confessions do not satisfy the soul's cravings in the ultimate analysis, which brings us to the bedrock of Hawthorne's quest—the human heart, where alone one could confront the problem of good and evil:

> The heart, the heart—there was the little yet boundless sphere wherein existed the original wrong of which the crime and misery of this outward world were mere types. Purify that inward sphere, and the many shapes of evil that haunt the outward, and which seem almost our only realities, will turn to shadowy, phantoms and vanish of their own accord.[5]

Thus individual reform lays in purification of the heart, further Hawthorne's concept of salvation was not strictly puritanical.

Immortality was a universal hope, not elective. There was no Heaven or Hell in the strict Biblical sense not even Judgement Day: "Man's only inexorable judge will be himself" and the punishment of his sins would be his perception of them. The experience of committing Sin was thus a prerequisite for growth. The greatest works of Hawthorne deal with the educative, humanising and regenerative power of Sin.

Sin is analysed against the background of a prohibitive social ethos. The framework is most often seventeenth-century New England. Eric Mottam comments:

> Seventeenth Century New England Society can be used as the instance of a group which knows it is corrupt but knows, too, that short of prayer, penitence and Jeremiads, it is condemned to the Manichean battlefield, the prior inhuman system of God and Devil. Life polarized into punishment and blessing, confession and concealment, marks the presence of the repressed in continuous dialectic with the public surfaces, partly euphoric drive and partly exhausting depression.[6]

In Hawthorne's works, seventeenth-century New England is shown as being synonymous with social repression which uses psychic repression in order to make the subjects docile. Deleuze and Guattari underline the process. "What really takes place is that the Law prohibits something that is perfectly fictitious in the order of desire or of the 'instincts' so as to persuade its subjects that they had the intention corresponding to this fiction. This is indeed the only way the law has of getting a grip on intention, of making the unconscious guilty."[7] A perfect example would be the casual plot of Hester Prynne's obedience and disobedience between the law of marriage and the transcendental law of erotic desire with a "consecration of its own." Hawthorne thus probes into the conscience of his characters. Hester Prynne, the adulteress who is punished in *The Scarlet Letter,* is followed in every imperceptible movement of her psychological progress; her proud but desperate isolation. Her slow reconquest of society, the renewed outbreak of feelings after years of expiation and finally, her passion for Reverend Dimmesdale reappears with undiminished strength, besides her Natural dignity, which is apparent after the pastor's death. Nina Baym comments:

> In Hester Prynne, Hawthorne created the first true heroine of American fiction, as well as one of its enduring heroes. Hester is a heroine because she is deeply implicated in, and responsive to, the gender structure of her society, and because her story, turning on "love" is "appropriate" for a woman. She is a hero because she has qualities and actions that transcend this gender reference and lead to heroism as it can be understood for any one.[8]

To a certain extent, Hester Prynne is more sinned against than sinning. Trapped in a loveless marriage with Roger Chillingworth, betrayed in her quest for personal happiness, an alien in Massachusetts. Hester Prynne is a ripe victim of the puritan psychosis. Her affair with the Reverend Arthur Dimmesdale, its offshoot, the love child Pearl, finds Hester having crossed over to no man's land and publicly branded an adulteress. She had committed the original sin, further, she had refused to divulge the name of her child's father. Taking upon herself the public humiliation and mortification of having to wear the "Scarlet Letter." The "A" signifies, at this point in time, "adulteress." However, in keeping with Hawthorne's symbolism, the letter and its significance are radically altered by the end of the novel. Although publicly condemned, Hester Prynne feels morally ratified. She loved Arthur Dimmesdale. The child was a product of their loving union. How, then, could it be wrong? As a direct indictment against the puritan rationale, Hawthorne shyly suggests an alternative judgement:

> Man had marked this woman's sin by a scarlet letter, which had such potent and disastrous efficacy that no human sympathy could reach her, save it were sinful like herself. God, as a direct consequence of the sin which man thus punished, had given her a lovely child, whose place was in that same dishonoured bosom, to connect her parent

> forever with the race and descent of mortals, and to be finally on blessed soul in heaven.[9]

There is in Hester Prynne a persistent individualism. She stays on in Boston on account of Dimmesdale and dedicates her life to bringing up Pearl. She is a devoted mother, meekly accepting the taunts and cruelty of her fellow men. Shunning the road to witchcraft on account of Pearl, she likewise rejects Anne Hutchinson's radical path for the same reasons. "Sin" being Hawthorne's special forte, he delves into the regenerative power of sin. Hester Prynne accepts the social condemnation of her adultery and pays the price. Gradually she grows more and more alienated and as she withdraws from the social concourse, she begins a journey inwards—which places her far beyond her time and age. The puritan code of ethics to which she paid allegiance was no longer hers. "The World's Law was no law for her mind." She was born ahead of her time and "She assumed a freedom of speculation, then common enough on the other side of the Atlantic but which our forefathers, had they knew it, would have held to be a deadlier crime than that stigmatized by the Scarlet Letter.[10]

Sin, as Hawthorne tacitly suggests in *The Scarlet Letter,* was the bedrock of puritanism. It was at once an individual and social aspect. Eric Mottram in his perceptive essay "Power and Law in Hawthorne's Fiction" comments: "So the monster created by a society or by and through its invented Gods—and this is a major basis of all fiction since Defoe, and cuts across the genres—elicits sympathy because he or she or it is the form of the repressed and oppressed. The illegal becomes a category of necessity and therefore strangely legal."[11] The individual and social perceptions of sin are exhaustively analysed by Hawthorne. Having gone beyond the pale of social mores, Hester Prynne graduates to individual freedom. When fate throws Arthur Dimmesdale across her path, she is prepared to fly into exile with him and the love child—Pearl. She only pays outward obedience to a system which has no further power upon her spirit. Hester Prynne is a fine example of Felix Culpa—"the fortunate fall," *i.e.* out of sin and evil comes good. Thus, Hester is educated and refined by her "wrong" doing. She awakens to a higher dispensation. In the forest scene of Chapter XVI-XIX, the sunshine bursts over Hester and Dimmesdale, "as with a smile of heaven." She even discards the Scarlet Letter, albeit temporarily. In keeping with her new perceptions, she has hopes of happiness in a life beyond death. She asks a dying Dimmesdale, "shall we not meet again...shall we not spend our immortal life together?"[12] But unlike her, he is still held by terrors of unpardonable sin: "The Law we broke!—the sin here so awfully revealed!—let these alone be in thy thoughts! fear!"[13] Hester has a further advantage over Dimmesdale. Having been proclaimed an adulteress and having been punished for it, she is comparatively free from the "Secret Sin" of concealment, unlike both Dimmesdale and Chillingworth. While the minister hides his sin, Chillingworth hides his identity. In Chapter III, Hester is confronted with her fellow adulterer, who is publicly called upon to persuade her as her spiritual guide to reveal his identity. Within Dimmesdale, there are twin urges—to hide and to be exposed. He pleads with Hester: "If thou feelest it to be for thy soul's peace, and that thy earthly punishment will therefore be made more effectual to salvation, I charge thee to speak out the name of thy fellow-sinner and fellow-sufferer."[14]

Dimmesdale provides a perfect foil to Hester, her partner in crime. Hawthorne's psychological probing into Dimmesdale is perhaps the finest portrait of a guilt-stricken conscience.

Hawthorne generally placed his characters in a position so as to wrestle with the problem of good and evil. Hester, by doing so, circumvents the problem, and gets above and beyond. The clue to Arthur Dimmesdale's character is that whereas Hester felt their love and its consequences were not a crime, Dimmesdale felt it was unforgivably wrong. While Hester is capable of great individuality and can stand alone, Dimmesdale comes across as heavily dependent on society. He is a by-product of the "puritan think." He needs to be endorsed and approved by society. This leads to a paradox within him. Since he depends on society, he cannot oppose its moral dictates, its allegiances, its rock-like justice. On the other hand, having committed a crime and having placed himself beyond the pale of society, he doubles his offence by not confessing to it. His need to be a great figure in public eyes keeps him silent over his personal limitations.

Hawthorne focuses upon the results of this duplicity. The inner agony and the need to suppress a gnawing conscience. Dimmesdale resorts to all sorts of pseudo tactics in order to still his puritan conscience. He carries out private penances, fasting, flagellation and ends up with nights without sleep. He often thinks of confession but even his public confessions are in a veiled symbolic language so as to remain obscure. In fact, the more aware he becomes of his limitations as a man, the greater is his power as a minister. His hypocrisy and subterfuge merely add to his glory:

> The minister well knew—subtle, but remorseful hypocrite that he was!—the light in which his vague confession would be viewed. He had striven to put a cheat upon himself by making the avowal of a guilty conscience, but had gained only one other sin, and a self-acknowledged shame, without the momentary relief of being self delivered. He had spoken the very truth, and transformed it into the veriest falsehood...[15]

If Arthur Dimmesdale was a mere charlatan, he would not cut a tragic figure. Unfortunately, his cowardice is coupled with qualities of the heart like compassion, sensitivity, intelligence, benevolence, a love of goodness and truth and an overwhelming unworldliness. This hiatus and discrepancy within him lead to his alienation. He loses touch with himself unlike Hester, whose experiences make her sink deeper and deeper within. Dimmesdale is lost in a world of shadows! "To the untrue man, the whole universe is false—it is impalpable—it shrinks to nothing within his grasp and he himself, in so far as he shows himself in a false light, becomes a shadow, or, indeed, ceases to exist."[16] The inner torment soon becomes visible on his face and the letter "A" emerges upon his chest. A modern-day equivalent would be *The Picture of Dorian Gray* by Oscar Wilde, wherein the inner essence stigmatizes the body or the portrait, as the case may be.

Dimmesdale literally sinks under the weight of his sin. It becomes the governing passion of his life. He is trapped within the past. His only purpose of existence is expiation for his sin: "The only truth, that continued to give Mr. Dimmesdale a real existence on this earth, was the anguish in his innermost soul, and the undissembled expression of it in his aspect...."[17]

His encounter with Hester in the forest and the tentative plan to escape with her and Pearl offer no respite. Dimmesdale's persecution complex is so deeply engraved so as to be only eased by death. In a sense, Arthur Dimmesdale is hounded to death by his dark Angel and physician Roger Chillingworth whose portrait is blood chilling and the vengeance he hopes to extract—horrific. Hawthorne came down heavily upon manipulative power and the evils of the predatory will, which cannot be eradicated because it is "evil." In his *American Notebooks,* he defined the unpardonable sin as a want of love and reverence for the Human Soul in consequence of which the investigator pried into the dark depths, not with hope or purpose of making it better, but from a cold philosophical curiosity which implies "a separation of the intellect from the heart." Thus Chillingworth's revenge which involves a violation in "cold blood" is a far greater crime than the sexual transgressions of Dimmesdale. Thus, in the ultimate analysis, his explicitly Mephistophelian design to cause Dimmesdale to die in a state of sin fails.

Chillingworth is an ambiguous character. He encounters his wife in a shocking manner. Separated from her by many vicissitudes, he comes upon her as she is dramatically exposed to public infamy. He makes an instantaneous decision, symbolised by the lifting of his finger to his lips to hide his tie to her. Thereafter he lives a double life, apparently harmless enough. In Chapter IV of *The Scarlet Letter,* Chillingworth, with great tenderness administers to Hester's sick baby, but she is appalled and terror-stricken: "Thy acts are like mercy. But thy words interpret thee as a terror...."[18] Masquerading as a physician he hides his diabolic intent, that of racking the minister's soul with constant anguish. Seemingly innocent he is a constant terror; "What Evil have I don the man?. I tell thee, Hester Prynne, the richest fee that ever physician earned from monarch could not have brought such care as I have wasted on this miserable priest."[19] He is always close upon the heels of Dimmesdale, even proposing to take passage on the same ship with the fleeing lovers. His endeavour at the end to keep Dimmesdale from a public confession at the scaffold could be interpreted as a friendly concern but is more akin to a devil struggling to snatch back an escaping soul. He speaks a Mephistophelian language, "All shall be well! Do not blacken your fame, and perish in dishonour. I can yet save you! Would you bring infamy on your sacred profession?"[20] Roger Chillingworth, however, has to contend with an Aristotelian reversal where a deep laid plan brings about an unforeseen and opposite reaction. It is only when Dimmesdale resists the evil posed by Roger Chillingworth that he openly reveals his purpose. This is followed by a terrible self-revelation that in condemning Arthur Dimmesdale, he himself has fallen into Damnation, "A mortal man, with once a human heart, has become a friend for his special torment."[21] The victim, Arthur Dimmesdale is forced to live a perpetual lie in public and his masochistic tendencies are augmented by the efforts of Chillingworth. Dimmesdale's torture lies in the fact that his perception of his personal sin is proportionate to his public virtue. His attempts at confession merely confuse the issue because of its veiled and metaphoric language. Even his great election day sermon seems to listeners to be divinely inspired and they are aware of the undertone of suffering and grief, which somehow seems universal in its impact: "...the complaint of a human heart, sorrow-laden, perchance guilty, telling the secret, whether of guilt or sorrow, to the great heart of mankind..."[22] Having lived a life of hypocrisy, it is only fitting that even in death his act of confession is misunderstood. And many "responsible witnesses" interpret his death as a culminating act of holiness and humility.

Thus, in keeping with Hawthorne's highly symbolic narration, the cultivated facade of Dimmesdale cannot be ruptured. Vice masquerading as Virtue builds an edifice of Good, difficult to tear down. Hester Prynne, *i.e.,* Virtue tainted with Vice likewise undergoes a transformation. *The Scarlet Letter* implying "Adultery" changes to "Able." Both Dimmesdale and Hester gain in status. In a social context, both attain a degree of eminence towards the end of the novel. Dimmesdale and Hester transgress the Puritan code. The former repents and the latter expiates. Thus, in the ultimate analysis, absolution is implied. In keeping with the nature of evil, which needs to "feed" upon something,

Roger Chillingworth decays and disintegrates once his mainstay Arthur Dimmesdale is dead. This exploitation of individuals for perverse purposes is a popular theme in Hawthorne's fiction. Aylmer, Rappacini and Ethan Brand likewise manipulate energy, human and non-human for their own vicarious ends. Their victims are as varied as Georgiana, Beatrice and Esther. Eric Mottram comments:

> Hawthorne is well aware that interference with another self infers the presence of the Unpardonable Sin, immediately the process becomes sheer usage for production—a perverse desire to move in on someone's life and use it, perhaps use it up.[23]

The only redeeming factor about Chillingworth is that he does the decent bourgeois thing of bequeathing Pearl enough property "both here and in England" to make her "the riches heiress of her day." In Hawthorne's fiction, there is a definite gradation of sorts; while characters of the heart like Hester and Dimmesdale circumvent the "mystery of ubiquity" albeit at a personal cost, characters of the head like Roger Chillingworth, the diabolic Westervelt and Hollingworth (*Blithedale Romance*), are beyond salvation.

Having analysed the *modus operandi* of individual sin, Hawthorne delves into a related problem of the "Sins of the Fathers" being visited upon the children. In this, Hawthorne looks ahead to Henrik Ibsen's *Ghosts*. The role of Pearl in *The Scarlet Letter* is purely symbolic and it is only towards the end of the novel that she is properly humanized. The first important factor about Pearl is that she is intrinsically linked with the Scarlet Letter, she is its living embodiment, "It was the Scarlet Letter in another form; the Scarlet Letter endowed with life."[24] Right from her early childhood, Pearl seems to reflect the Scarlet Letter in her choice of colours and adornments. She mirrors in some way Hester Prynne. At this early stage in the novel, she is more her mother's child than her father's daughter. Hester recognizes in Pearl's character, the "warfare" of her own spirit during her pregnancy: "She could recognize her wild, desperate, defiant mood, the flightiness of her temper and even some of the very cloud-shapes of gloom and despondency that had brooded in her heart."[25] Pearl is, above all, a by-product of a sexual transgression. Thus she combines in her person qualities of extreme freedom as well as waywardness:

> The child could not be made amenable to rules. In giving her existence, a great law had been broken; and the result was a being, whose elements were perhaps beautiful and brilliant, but all in disorder.[26]

The child was conceived by breaking the puritan code of morality. Thus, she possesses qualities antithetical to the rigid Puritans. She is beautiful, intelligent, perfectly shaped, vigorous, graceful, passionate, imaginative, impulsive, capricious, creative and visionary. These qualities in Pearl are also qualities in Hester Prynne. She is almost her "double"—her *alter ego* even. The child's lawlessness shows up Hester's true nature below her outwardly subservient public demeanour.

Pearl also has a special and original relation to the Scarlet Letter. The purpose of Pearl in the novel is dual. The child represents elements of defiant and lawless beauty. She also is a form of conscience. She symbolizes both her mother's guilt as well as her rebellion. She is responsible for keeping the Scarlet Letter firmly in her mother's mind and eyes. This is clearly seen in the forest scene when Hester throws away the Scarlet Letter. Pearl, however, refuses to join her until the letter is restored to its rightful place. Symbolically this could only imply that the reputation of the letter implies a repudiation of Pearl. Pearl grows up surrounded by patriarchs, authorities, rulers and father figures, but she truly lacks a father. It is only towards the end of the novel when she kisses a dying Dimmesdale that she becomes fully humanized:

> A spell was broken. The great scene of grief, in which the wild infant bore a part, had developed all her sympathies; and as her tears fed upon her father's cheek, they were the pledge that she would grow up amid human joy and sorrow, not forever do battle with the world, but be a woman in it. Towards her mother, too, Pearl's errand as a messenger of anguish was fulfilled.[27]

Pearl lacks identity throughout the novel. It is only in her father's public act of recognition and acknowledgement that she truly finds her roots and is placed beyond the pale of the Puritan society of which she symbolized merely a broken law. In the narrow puritan ethos, Pearl is a victim who finally emerges as a victor, having wiped the Boston dusk off her feet.

To Hawthorne, the sense of ancestral sin was a palpable reality. He maintained: "It is a terrible thought, that an individual wrong-doing melts into the great mass of human crime, and makes us...guilty of the whole."[28] Richard Harter Fogle in his perceptive book *Hawthorne's Fiction: The Light and Dark* (1952) comments:

> As with *The Scarlet Letter*, *The House of the Seven Gables* is concerned with the effects of an evil action, this time prolonged over generations. As in *The Scarlet Letter*, the act cannot be recalled—in this world there is no annulment, no wiping the slate clean until the original sin was worked itself out.[29]

Historically, *The House of the Seven Gables* looks back to a dark period in American history vis-à-vis the Salem Witch trials when Puritan America was caught in the hysteria of witch hunting. The trial of the so-called witches was often a mere farce, the evidence flimsy and weighed down by superstition. The great Puritan ministers were all in all. Cotton Mather's book *The Wonders of the Invisible World* exonerates the judges for the murder and torture of supposed witches. Witchcraft was a widely accepted phenomenon in that seventeenth-century Europe and America. The Puritans felt that disbelief in witchcraft seemed to question the existence of God. The admission of "Spectral" influence was likewise effective. Cotton Mather had presided once a number of trials and was responsible for the infliction of many horrendous punishments. To the modern reader, excerpts from *Wonders of the Invisible World* seem lopsided, smacking of mob hysteria rather than factual court trials, for example, there is the case of Bridget Bishop alias Oliver who was condemned as a witch and whose trial was held at the court of Dyer and Terminer at Salem, June 2, 1692. She had been accused of possessing an evil eye:

> It was testify'd, that at the Examination of the Prisoner before the Magistrates, the Bewitched were extremely Tortured. If she did cast her Eyes on Them, they were presently struck down; and this in such a manner as there could be no collusion in the Business. But upon the Touch of her Hand upon them, when they lay in their swoons, they would immediately Revive; and not upon the Touch of anyones else. Moreover, upon some Special actions of her Body as the shaking of her Head or the turning of her Eyes, they presently and painfully fell into the like postures. And many of the like Accidents now fell out, while she was at the Bar. One of the same testifying, that she said, she could not be troubled to see the Afflicted thus Tormented.[30]

On these and other equally insufficient grounds, Bridget Bishop of Salem Village was the first witch to be tried (June 2) and executed (June 10). Thereafter the death penalty accorded for convictions in witchcraft was common enough. Hawthorne was likewise aware that several of his ancestors had figured prominently in the Witch trials. Perhaps it was the desire to lay down the burden of ancestral guilt that made him write *The House of the Seven Gables*. The theme of the novel is puritan enough that of ancestral sin, but the effect is that of tragedy akin to the House of Atreus, where one blind act of wrong leads to another and yet another, destroying several generations. *The House of the Seven Gables* equals the brooding intensity of Edgar Allen Poe's *The Fall of the House of Usher*.

In *The House of the Seven Gables,* Hawthorne returns to his preoccupation of Sin, seen in the traditional conflict between good and evil. Built vaguely around the fictional retelling of Sara Good's curse on John Hawthorne "God will give you blood to drink." A helpless woman's curse against her Judge and tormentor is synonymous with Maule's curses which affect the nineteenth-century descendants of Pyncheon: "The germ which may and must produce good or evil fruit."[31] The result of the curse is inevitable and it is a doomed house we see on Pyncheon Street. Colonel Pyncheon had Matthew Maule accused and executed for witchcraft in order to gain his land. In this manner, the influential class tyrannized over the common man: "Clergyman, judges, statesman—the wisest, calmest, holiest persons of their day—stood in the inner circle round about the gallows, loudest to applaud the work of blood, latest to confess themselves miserably deceived."[32] The principal characters of *The House of the Seven Gables* are Hepzibah, Clifford, Phoebe and Judge, Pyncheon and Holgrave. Hepzibah is of the true blue blood Pyncheon Stock. As the heroine of the book, she is a symbol and a victim of the old order. Sheltered and weakened by its unbiased gentility. Forced by circumstances to do the unseemly thing of keeping a "cent shop." She is a grotesque unattractive old maid, a soul led astray, wandering in a maze, estranged from life by inherited and vicarious guilt. Hepzibah and her unfortunate brother Clifford are both victims. Clifford, a creature of pure aesthetic sensibility has been mutilated by contact with the Pyncheon curse. Exquisitely fitted to appreciate all that is pleasant in life, he is reduced to a mental wreck, having spent several years in prison. The man responsible for his entombment being none other than his cousin Jeffrey. The far-reaching effects of the Maule curse turn the Pyncheons upon each other.

The "curse" is no doubt a major factor in the novel but no less so is the "Sin" of the Pyncheons. The "Sin" being as old as Lucifer, the archetypal downfall due to pride. Through pride, the Pyncheons sought to isolate themselves. Under the delusion of their own greatness, they "fall." The Maule's, the "underdogs" have thrived to triumph eventually. Their forbearance, courage and humility have seen them through. The pride of the Pyncheons symbolised by the House of the Seven Gables is built by Maule's labour on Maule's land, now in possession of the Pyncheons. But the victims get the better of their masters. The builder of the house of the Seven Gables, the son of Matthew Maule, hides the documents of the Eastern lands, the token of the unbounded wealth of the Pyncheons. Thus the Maules keep a hold on Pyncheons. In fact, legend had it that the lowly Maules held the Pyncheons in thrall in the world of dreams, "the topsy-turvy common wealth of sleep." The mesmerizing powers of the Maule are responsible for the destruction of one Pyncheon—Alice Pyncheon. Holgrave, the modern-day descendant of the Maules likewise exercises a hypnotic control over Phoebe, the present Pyncheon, but desists because he loved her, thereby showing the control of the head by the heart.

Speaking about the heart naturally enough reminds us of Phoebe Pyncheon. Richard Harter Fogle comments:

> Phoebe Pyncheon is the closest to the center of human nature. A conservative in the best sense. She represents the truth of the heart. She is the best of humanities and human feeling. She has far less moral depth than Hepzibah, to whom she is as a child to a woman; she is less sensitive than Clifford, and much less intelligent than Holgrave; but Hawthorne represents her as of greater power than any of these, through instinctive but consummate talent for everyday living.[33]

Phoebe Pyncheon, who is responsible for the redemption of the last of the Pyncheons, is no thoroughbred product. She does not have a direct line of descent. She has been isolated from the Pyncheon influence since her father married a young woman "of no family or property" and died in very poor circumstances. However, it is Phoebe who is selected to carry on the thread of continuity. Her marriage to Holgrave is indication enough. Holgrave is the "new man," the radical democrat, a member of the Maule family. It is in her alliance with him that the Pyncheon line continues to purge the ancient curse and the "sin" of pride. The slate can only be wiped clean when the original sin has worked itself out. The sin of Colonel Pyncheon was greed and his desire to enrich his descendants, but instead, he brought the curse upon them. Clifford and Hepzibah Pyncheon separated by many generations from the Puritan colonel, suffer the greater part of their lives in expiation.

The house Itself is an enduring symbol. The house and the family are interchangeable: "The aspect of the venerable mansion has always affected me like a human countenance, bearing traces not merely of outward storm and sunshine, but expressive, also, of the long lapse of mortal life, and accompanying vicissitudes that have passed within."[34] It is like a living sentient organism, "like a great human heart." The Pyncheon past has not been all bad. The long history of human habitation has left its mark. The house is "Weather-beaten." The "green moss" gives the house a softening grace. But the giant burdocks with "enormous fertility" are ominous and unwholesome. Further, there hangs over the house a sense of the past, it smacks of dust and decay, "unwholesome for the lungs." Phoebe alone combats the sordid grime, its dry rot, its "heavy, breathless scent." Over the physical decay, there is an overhanging sense of wrong-doing and spiritual stagnation. Clifford finds it reeking of death, "a rusty, crazy, dry-rotted, damp-rotted, dingy, dark and miserable old dungeon."[35]

The upper section of the house projects over the lower section casting a "thoughtful gloom" over the whole edifice. The only mitigating factor is Alice's Poesies which grow high up between the gables, thereby suggesting a link with nature and a possibility of redemption. At the end of the novel, the flowers indicate the passing of the curse! "They were flaunting in rich beauty and full bloom today and seemed, as it were, a mystic expression that something within the house was consummated."[36]

The garden, likewise, is associated with the Pyncheons and shows the simultaneous effect of both good and evil. It is Eden suitably tainted. Its rich black earth has a flavour of the Churchyard and the Sexton's spade. The beautiful white roses have mildew at heart. Besides, there is the Maule Well, whose water was once sweet, now "bewitched" and dangerous to drink. As always with Hawthorne, the influence of Nature is benign even in a blighted place. The bees come and they visit the garden. Its decay is arrested by the combined efforts of Phoebe and Holgrave, uprooting the weeds and planting more wholesome seedlings. On her first visit to the garden, Phoebe notices the results of Holgrave's attempts to stem the rot:

> The evil of these departed years would naturally have sprung up again, in such rank weeds, as are always prone to root themselves about human dwellings. Phoebe, saw however, that their growth must have been checked by a degree of careful labour, bestowed daily and systematically on the garden.[37]

Symbolically the uprooted weeds would imply the transmitted vices of society. Like the garden, Clifford and Hepzibah have been victimised and akin to Holgrave's efforts with the garden, we have Phoebe's effort to reclaim Hepzibah and Clifford.

The interior of the house likewise reflects the stern cold inexorable quality of puritan laws. Especially so in the chair, portrait and chamber of the old Colonel—all of which is infused with darkness. The portrait symbolised an evil influence "so darkly to mingle the shadows of their presence with the sunshine of the passing hour, that no good thoughts or purpose could ever spring up and blossom here."[38] Even the chair is straight backed and stiff, ingeniously contrived for the discomfort of people and irksome to the sight. The chair conveys "the ugliest, possible idea" of the state of society to which they could have been adapted. Whatever dignity the house of the Seven Gables has been able to muster up is belied by the little cent shop beneath its front gable. Its shop bell rings out in mockery against the pride and pretensions of the Pyncheon past. Hepzibah is forced by circumstances to keep a cent shop which had been constructed by an ancestor, who, ignoring the ducal history of the house had become a shopkeeper.

The Pyncheons have one and all been passing on a pipe dream of amassing fortunes based on the realization of territorial rights. The "Shop", however, shows their Achilles' heel, the chink in their armour. They have lived above their means in dubious pomp and splendour, hence their straightened circumstances. As against the aristocratic Pyncheons, the Maules are plebeians, for example carpenters, artisans and sailors before the mast. Their continuity is subterranean. Matthew Maule's posterity is now supposed to be extinct. "For thirty years past, neither town-record, nor gravestone, nor the directory, nor the knowledge or memory of man bore any trace of Matthew Maule's descendants."[39] Like the Phoenix, they rise from the ashes. Unlike the Pyncheons, they are capable of regeneration. They rise with renewed vigour in the person of Holgrave, the daguerreotypist tenant in *The House of the Seven Gables*. Holgrave is the "new man" possessing more intellect than heart. He is radical in his views and has his share of intellectual shortcomings. He is a typical Yankee who has dabbled in every trade by the age of twenty-two. He has been a salesman, a school master, an editor, a peddler, a dentist, a super cargo, a Fourierist, a lecturer of mesmerism and finally, a daguerreotypist. He is saved from going the way of Ethan Brand, or Hollingworth or even Roger Chillingworth because of his love for Phoebe. Holgrave's brand of radicalism seeks to purify with fire the house of the Seven Gables "till only its ashes remain." The Maules, unlike the Pyncheons, had to rough it out; more often than not, ending their lives in alms houses. They live obscure lives with hired tenants. Compared to the Pyncheons, they are rootless. Never daring to aspire to any such symbol of possession as the House of the Seven Gables. Although belonging to the dregs of society, there is something that sets the Maules apart from the common man, they are isolated and are tainted by the "Wizard's" blood, having acquired "a hereditary character of reserve." Richard Harter Fogle comments: "This reserve is a product of the original crime against them and is imposed upon them rather than innate. Thus, it is another instance of the complexity of Hawthorne's moral situations in which the guiltless victims as well as the criminals suffer spiritual harm."[40] The Maules, who were more sinned against than sinning, are ripe for regeneration having thrived in adversity. The Pyncheons, on the other hand, are puffed up by spiritual pride, of which their greed is both the symptom and the instrument. The penalty of their sin is a materialistic delusion centering itself in their claim upon the Eastern Lands of Waldo County, Maine, which for generations filled them with false aspirations:

> This impalpable claim...resulted in nothing more solid than to cherish, from generation to generation, and absurd delusion of family importance, which all along characterised by Pyncheons.[41]

Thus, the Phantom of immeasurable wealth makes the Pyncheons live above their means, resulting in their impoverishment.

Clifford and Hepzibah are blighted by Maule's curse and incarcerated within the house, which offers them no viable escape. One remarkable feature of the house is the arched window which overlooks the street from the second storey. The window is the only passage to the greater world. Clifford views the pageantry of life from this window, from which he is isolated, "a mighty river of life...calling to the kindred depth within him." He even contemplates plunging suicidally into the surging stream. The Pyncheons are trapped within the confines of the past. An evil past, of which the house is a comprehensive symbol. At one point, Clifford and Hepzibah try to escape from the house, leaving the Church, they try to merge with the crowd. But scarcely past their door, they are filled with revulsion and take refuge in the very mansion they hate. The shock of the death of the Judge drives them so far as to take a train. Clifford is almost deranged, exhilarated by the release. Their freedom is short-lived, "The freedom of a broken law." Clifford's bubble bursts when they pass a darkened, decayed Church and an old farmhouse. Inescapable reminders to the Pyncheons that the past is inescapable.

In Hawthorne's allegorical conflict between good and evil, both sides are evenly poised. Thus the two strong men in the book are Holgrave and Jeffrey Pyncheon. While Holgrave's urge to power is controlled by fundamental morality, the Judge's lust for the material is unqualified by humanity. The judge is a die-hard Pyncheon and possesses the insatiable greed of his ancestors, therein he repents the original sin of the Pyncheons. Judge Pyncheon is led on a wild goose chase in search of money, thanks to an ambiguous remark of Clifford. Having destroyed Clifford, the Judge tries to browbeat Hepzibah and Phoebe. His destruction towards the end of the novel is an act of fate. Therein he partakes of the curse against the first Pyncheon. The darkness of the house in which the dead judge sits is symbolic. The darkness is evil, accentuated by the storm brought in by the east wind, slowly the darkness fades, and the wind veers to the northwest. The induction of starlight and the "Silvery dance" of the moonbeams indicates the clearing of the moral atmosphere. As always with Hawthorne, there is the ultimate triumph of good over evil, albeit at a cost.

This admixture of good and evil is a very fine, delicate one. Holgrave, the "new man," possesses flaws as well as virtues. In his haste to bring about change, he would destroy much that is good along with the evil. His brand of radicalism has to be tempered with mercy. Hawthorne elsewhere has been critical of pure creatures of the head. Holgrave has his share of intellectual shortcomings. His well-meant universal philanthropy would eradicate all human warmth, idiosyncrasies and relationships. He is speculative, prone to wander far from the safe center of things. He has more than a hint of cold analytical curiosity of Ethan Brand, which could lead to the unpardonable sin. Further, he is prone to view the emotions and sorrows of Clifford and Hepzibah as a mere intellectual treat (Ref: Miles Coverdale in the *Blithedale Romance*). Besides his curiosity, he possesses the gift of mesmerism, which for Hawthorne, constituted a violation of the human spirit. Hawthorne has increasingly dealt with such characters in his fiction. Matthew Maule destroyed Alice Pyncheon. While Zenobia in the *Blithedale Romance* likewise uses her powers. However, therein Holgrave is superior, he does not succumb to the temptation of using his power over Phoebe to his advantage.

Thus, Holgrave is redeemed by the qualities of the heart—the sincerity of his love for Phoebe. Thus, in Holgrave the heart wins over the head. The Maule marries the Pyncheon, bringing to an end the sufferings occasioned by the sins of the fathers. Balance and tranquility are restored after several generations, have paid the price and original sin, weeded out. With the death of Judge Pyncheon, the Maule curse is effectively at an end. The past is wiped out, paid for, heralding a new beginning.

Having toyed with the devastating effects of individual sin in *The Scarlet Letter* and the prolonged effects of sin over generations in *The House of the Seven Gables*, Hawthorne moved on to the novel concept of Utopia and its practical impossibility in the *Blithedale Romance*. Utopianism was very much a part of the American Dream, since the earliest colonization of America spelled the possibility of the realization of Utopias. There was a Utopian aspect in the original settlement of the eastern seaboard as well as in the later westward expression. In the words of George Norlin, the Americans:

> have been, for the most part, dissenters and non conformists with rebellion in their blood. They came overseas to these

> un-preempted shores as refugees from the inhibitions and disabilities of established orders in their home countries whose oppressions they had not been able to shake off. Theirs was a flight from restraint....[42]

In keeping with the American spirit, emigrants to America were not merely refugees from facts but were voyagers to ideas. Calvinism with its desire to form a New Jerusalem in America was not very successful. This was because of its not-so-attractive pessimistic and deterministic aspects. The ascendant star in the horizon was transcendentalism with its exuberant optimism. Historically, the period of Jackson favoured democracy over social and intellectual aristocracy. Philanthropists like Robert Owen sought to turn America into the land of millennial promise. Utopianism inspired a movement towards reform. Mere flight from restraint would imply anarchy but a Utopia required a dynamic unifying idea that can subdue and harmonize divergent wills it carried along. The Americans desired to inspire individuals to a larger life through establishing conditions favourable to their intellectual and moral improvement. O.B. Frothingham qualifies the spirit of the age by pointing out that:

> New England furnished the only plot of ground on this planet, where the transcendental philosophy had a chance to show what it was and what it proposed. The forms of life there were, in a measure, plastic. There were not immovable prejudices, no fixed and unalterable traditions....No orders of men, no aristocracies of intellect, no privileged classes of thought were established. A feeling was abroad that all things must be new in the new world. There was call for immediate application of ideas to life.[43]

Unfortunately, the Utopia proved short-lived. The reality did not support Utopias, as is clearly evinced by the failure of Robert Owen's New Harmony, Indiana. Francis Wrights's Nashoba, Tennessee and the transcendental experiment at Brook Farm established in 1840 proved a dismal failure. A disillusioned Margaret Fuller confessed: "The criticism and attack on institutions, and external ills,...sees at last that the only efficient remedy must come from individual character."[44]

Nathaniel Hawthorne likewise had his share of the transcendental experiment at Brook Farm, having lived there for a little more than half a year from April to November 1841. A decade later, he wrote the *Blithedale Romance* based on his experience at Brook Farm. However, as Henry James has pointed out, it was "merely a perch for starting upon an imaginative fight."[45] The *Blithedale Romance* is a hybrid production, part romance and part social commentary. It is, above all, an expose of Utopian ideology. As with all Hawthorne's work, the analogy of good and evil is carried on, with Zenobia as the witch figure and Priscilla as the white innocent figure.

The *Blithedale Romance* is the only one of Hawthorne's four major romances written in the first person. The narrator Miles Coverdale, an old bachelor, is recollecting events that have taken place in his youth. As a young man, Coverdale had joined the Blithedale community, fired by a desire for social reform. Above all, he sought to create poetry. "I hope now, to produce something that shall really deserve to be called poetry— true, strong, natural and sweet, as is the life which we are going to lead...."[46] But the noble motives are merely a camouflage for his voyeuristic tendencies. In "Lights from a Steeple," there is a similar rationale for morbid curiosity:

> The most desirable mode of existence might be that of a spiritualized Paul Pry, hovering invisible round man and woman, witnessing their deeds, searching into their hearts, borrowing brightness from their felicity and shade from their sorrow, and retaining no emotion peculiar to himself.[47]

Coverdale indulges in his curiosity unobserved from his leafy tree-top "hermitage" and the boarding house window in the town from which he could see into Zenobia's hotel room opposite. He further observes the dramatic conflicts between other people as unobtrusively as possible. He condones his wrong doing on the ground that he has sympathy for the people observed and sought to give the immutability of lives. The permanence of art: "My own part in these transactions was singularly subordinate. It resembled that of the chorus in a classic play, which seems to be set apart from personal concern, and bestows the whole measure of its hope or fear, its exultation or sorrow, on the fortunes of others, between whom and itself this sympathy is its only bond."[48] His protestations lack sincerity and purpose. His desire that the Blithedale community figure historically in an "epic poem" appears nonsense to Hollingworth who realises Miles Coverdale is not in earnest, "either as a poet or a Laborer."

Coverdale is especially interested in the sensuous Zenobia and probes into her relation with Hollingworth, the reformer and Priscilla, her sister. Zenobia resents his scrutiny and rebukes him often enough. "You know not what you do! It is dangerous, Sir, believe me, to tamper thus with earnest human passions, out of your own mere idleness and for your sport. I will endure it no longer!"[49] Coverdale, however, continues with his voyeuristic tendencies, claiming that he did so out of an "uncertain sense of duty." Zenobia, in turn, lashes out at the cold-blooded curiosity of the artist, which seeks to play games with human emotions for one's own personal satisfaction: "a cold-blooded criticism, founded on a shallow interpretation of half perceptions, a monstrous scepticism in regard to any conscience or any wisdom, except one's own; a most irreverent propensity to thrust Providence aside, and substitute oneself in its awful place—out of these, and comes your idea of duty."[50] She realises that the artist seeks to poetise reality, never present the naked truth. Before her desperate suicide having been rejected by Hollingworth, she tells Coverdale "you are turning this whole affair into a ballad. By all means write this ballad, and turn your sympathy to good account, as other poets do, and poets must unless they choose to give us glittering icicles instead of lives of fire."[51] Coverdale likewise probes into Priscilla, "I could not resist the impulse to take on peep beneath her folded petals." He also manages to pry out the secret of old Moodie, the father of the two sisters. All this inquisitiveness has been taking a toll of Coverdale. He has been turning slowly but immeasurably into a fiend—cold-hearted beyond endurance. A similar sketch of an artist is to be found in *The Prophetic Pictures* published sixteen years before the *Blithedale Romance:*

> Like all other men around whom an engrossing purpose wreathes itself, he was insulated from the mass of humankind. He had no aim—no pleasure— no sympathies—but what was ultimately connected with his art. Though gentle in manner, and upright in intent and action, he did not possess kindly feelings; his heat was cold; no living creature could be brought near enough to keep him warm.[52]

The outcome of this morbid curiosity is that Coverdale is left with a guilt-stricken sense of responsibility for the tragic outcome of events into which he had pried and intruded. As he confesses, the later years turn out to be "all an emptiness." The artist disintegrates with the subject of his art. In quite the same way, in a different situation, Roger Chillingworth sort of crumbles once the object of his scrutiny Arthur Dimmesdale is dead. Roy R. Male comments: "Coverdale is what Hawthorne feared he might have become if he had not given himself in love and marriage."[53]

The *Blithedale Romance* reads not merely as an indictment of the artist but of the reformer as well. Hollingworth is equipped with admirable traits and good intentions. But unfortunately, he is unappreciative of artistic concerns. He has no "external polish" and "courtesy of manner" but more than makes up with "a tenderness in his voice, eyes, mouth, in his gesture, and in every indescribable manifestation, which few men could resist, and no women."[54] Hollingworth is a reformer with a zeal, and his cherished project of establishing an institution for the reformation is laudable enough. But the zeal turns to fanaticism and intolerance of differences of opinion, his virtue becomes his vice. His compassion is perverted by self-interest. His solicitous attendance at Coverdale's sick bed appears in hindsight to be motivated by self-interest: Coverdale wonders whether he had attended on him with the sole purpose of making him "a proselyte to his views." Hollingworth's rise from toil and obscurity, while it helped him understand the labouring classes, it made him impatient with matters beyond his understanding. He condemned Coverdale's poetry as idle frippery and Zenobia for her interest in matters beyond his comprehension. Darrel

Abel comments: "The failure of imagination is Hawthorne's way of indicating that, philanthropic optimism is more likely to be a characteristic of unenlightened, half-educated persons than those with cultivation and greater knowledge of life."[55] Hawthorne's personal experience in Brook Farm convinced him that manual labour was incompatible with artistic activity. The Brook Farm experiment was aimed primarily at effecting a natural union between "intellectual and manual labour." Bronson Alcott, who endured months of drudgery at Brook Farm, came to the conclusion that labour was the curse of the world, and nobody could meddle with it without becoming proportionally "brutified."

Hollingworth was determined to advance his own scheme of social reform and stoutly denied considering the merit of other equally desirable schemes of social advancement. Perhaps the most ugly facet of Hollingworth was that in spite of being a prominent member of the Blithedale community and aware of the deep involvement of the other members, Hollingworth privately called Blithedale "a wretched, insubstantial scheme." Intolerant of interference, he contemplated turning his friends off Blithedale Farm so that he could establish his pet project.

Most of Hawthorne's obsessive characters like Rappacini, Ethan Brand, Aylmer, Wakefield, and Richard Digby in the tales, Westervelt, Judge Pyncheon and Roger Chillingworth are deluded by appearances. Likewise, Hollingworth's obsessive desires make him incapable of being unmotivated even in his closest relationship. He contemplates marrying Zenobia so that her wealth could fund his projects. He, however, is scornful of the Fourierism she advocates and the equality of the sexes: "Woman is a monster...without man as her acknowledged principal."[56] Hollingworth's blindness to every truth but his own version and his desire to force compliance makes him an ignorant zealot rather than true reformer. In Hawthorne's fictional treatment of good and evil, Hollingworth is an example of philanthropy which works evil all around.

In "New England Reformers" Emerson comments:

> They are partial; they are not equal to the work they pretend. They lose their way; in their assault on the

> kingdom of darkness they expend all their energy on some accidental evil, and lose their sanity and power of benefit. It is of little moment that one or two or twenty errors of our social system be correlated but of much that the man be in his senses.[57]

The worst effect of his monomania was a perversion of personal relationships. He casts off Coverdale, and discards Zenobia when her wealth proves unavailable to finance his schemes. Hollingworth is aware of the disastrous effects of his conduct and relapses into impotent despondency. He remains, from first to last, in the words of Zenobia, "Self, Self, Self! You have embodied yourself in a project. You are a better masquerader than the witches and gypsies yonder; for your disguise is a self-deception."[58]

The Blithedale community had its fair share of Fourierists. Zenobia's advanced views show her to be a feminist ahead of her time. But like Hollingworth, she comes to a bitter end unlike Hester Prynne, whose "native energy of character" helped her overcome a traumatic history. Zenobia's passion betrays her, making her judgements untrustworthy. She had initially lavished her "dew drops" on the cynical Westervelt, who was incapable of a spiritual response to her passion. Coverdale realises that Zenobia's moral judgements have been perverted by her sexual aberrations: "The woman who swerves in a hair's breadth... out of the beaten track...with that one hair's breadth...goes all astray, and never sees the world in its true aspect afterwards."[59] Since Zenobia is insincere she cannot be an effective feminist. She even betrays her sister Priscilla into Westervelt's hands to be mesmerised as the veiled lady. Priscilla is one of Hawthorne's snow images. Like Phoebe, she is the incarnation of purity. Her physical frailty and spirituality are reinforced throughout the novel. In the proverbial clash of good and evil, the rivalry of the passionate and wilful Zenobia with the feeble Priscilla, Hawthorne hands the laurels of victory to Priscilla, who achieves the marital felicity her proud voluptuous sister contended for. Hollingworth rejects Zenobia for Priscilla. The sexually experienced woman pays the price. In the ultimate analysis, it is only the pure and innocent like Phoebe in the *Home of the Seven Gables* and Priscilla in *The Blithedale Romance,* who escape unscathed in Hawthorne's scheme of things. The temptresses like Hester Prynne in *The Scarlet Letter* or Miriam in *The Marble Faun* work out the "mystery of iniquity" albeit, at a high personal cost. Zenobia is not even given this satisfaction and is self-destructive. Hawthorne's obsession with sin and the problem of good and evil continued throughout his fictional life, but nowhere has it been presented in a more stark and dramatic manner than in *The Marble Faun.* Because of the profusion of allusions, symbols and images, *The Marble Faun* has often foxed critics. As Merle E. Brown puts it, this novel has been subjected to "a plethora of interpretations," no single one of which is especially satisfactory."[60] However, the most obvious motif in *Marble Faun* is the fall myth. "Felix-Culpa" or the fortunate fall, a theme which Hawthorne returned to in much of his fictional work.

Donatello and Miriam are Hawthorne's Adam and Eve. There is an added dimension to Donatello, who bears a striking resemblance to the antique Faun of Praxiteles. Donatello is almost completely a symbolic character. He is the natural man "in a high and beautiful sense, an animal." He also possesses the quality of prelapsarian innocence. The world as it exists to the apprehension of Donatello, the natural man is a garden Mote Beni, his ancestral home is a Paradisal Hill. The paradisal aspects of even the artificial Borghese garden become distinct and vivid in his presence.

Donatello shares many qualities with the Faun. He is innocent, his motives are sympathy and antipathy, not purpose and endeavour. He is sensuous and ageless, far from considerations of personal destiny. Another characteristic quality of the Faun is his amorality, preferring to follow natural instincts. In Faun, there is candor but no moral responsibility. His honesty is a mere outcome of his total simplicity. The Faun is, above all, a symbol of man's instinctive presence in Nature. Above all, Donatello's association with the Faun implies a blending of Art and Nature. As Donatello is to Adam, Miriam is to Eve. She is bewitching and "oriental" of mysterious origin. Her resemblance to Kenyon's statue of Cleopatra gives us a clue to her character.

She is the seductress, the temptress. Donatello would never have entered the Catacombs except for Miriam's "attractive influence." Having a distinct preference for light, he is repulsed by the gloomy regions. Later, Miriam beckons Donatello into the shadowy corner of her room. Finally, it is she who lures him from the world of innocence into the bondage of sin, into the darkest corner of darkness, when he heaves the body of the Spectre from Traitor's leap. Together Miriam and Donatello are "the beautiful man, the beautiful woman, united for ever..."[61] in crime which dissociates Donatello for ever from his innocent past. Like Eve, Miriam felt the need to make Donatello an accessory to the crime. The Spectre murdered by Donatello, haunting the Catacombs is subject to varied interpretations. The most relevant being that of Darrel Abel:

> So is the Spectre of the Catacomb (Miriam's model) a symbol of man's beguilement, into a world of abstractive thought. Instead of joyous participation, in the instant life of Nature, his existence is a gloomy isolation in an introspective egoism, his consciousness peopled by phantom from a remembered past.[62]

While the Faun is human nature among sunshine and flower to the unexplored cavern of the heart, the spectre is a monster, the terrible gloom within. While the Faun expresses man's delights in the vivid present and appeals to the senses, the Spectre represents the shadowy past. The world as it exists to the apprehension of the Spectre is a tomb. Donatello is a daylight creature, convinced of his own immortality: "why should it have any end? How long! Forever, forever, forever!"[63] The Spectre lives in the past. His relentless pursuit of Miriam typifies what Hawthorne described in "Monsieur du Miroir" as the hopeless race that men sometimes run "with memory on their own hearts, or their moral selves." The Spectre's intent is evil, he would gratify his fiendish malignity...by perhaps bringing some old pestilence or other forgotten and long-buried evil on society; or possibly, teaching the modern world some decayed and dusty kind of crime which the antique Romans knew, and then would hasten back to the catacomb.[64]

The Spectre sought to beguile victims into his own misery, that is, a withdrawal from life into his condition of self-love and sterile introspection.

Having been stained with the blood of murder, the Adam and Eve figures, Donatella and Miriam are shut out of paradise. After drinking a "marriage" toast at the Trevi fountain, they consummate a "union that consists in guilt."

Borghese Garden, the lost Eden, is the backdrop of Miriam's and Donatella's last dance of innocence, whose perfection is marred only by the intrusion of the Spectre:

> For due time, some mortal, whom they reverence too highly, is commissioned by Providence to teach them this direful lesson; he perpetuated a sin; and Adam falls anew, and Paradise, heretofore in unfaded bloom is lost again, and closed forever, with the fiery swords gleaming at its gates.[65]

However, the repercussions of sin do not inhere with the sinner alone, Hilda, a close friend and confidante of Miriam, sins by proxy: "every crime destroys more Edens than our own." In *The Marble Faun*, every character moves through a set pattern—from innocence to experience or knowledge of evil. Thereafter, there is a period of isolation, then repentance and the journey back to the center. While Donatello and Miriam undergo this transformation, which also implies an evolutionary leap from a lower to a higher conscience which is the adjustment the ego is required to make in the world, Hilda, however is unable to make the requisite change since she is unwilling to permit the knowledge of evil to enter her conscious mind. Hilda is good, but her goodness is carried to a degree where it is synonymous with evil—the evil of the isolated intellect. But Hilda differs from both Rappaccini and Ethan Brand. Rappaccini reverses the role of God and man. He produces pure beauty— his daughter and pure poison—his plants. God's world, however, admits of a mixture, that is, impurity in both the poison and in beauty. Hilda, however, does not produce anything, she merely sees things as pure and perfect and can see them no other way. Marius Bewley says: "Hilda loses her innocence by proxy, as it were when she sees her friends commit a crime."[66] There is evidence that Hilda is an inbred, tried and true puritan. While other characters of Hawthorne, like Aylmer, Peter Goldthwaite and Judge Pyncheon are materialists, Hilda is an idealist deluded by appearances. Hilda, the blond pure artist has every aspect of virginal purity. Miriam refers to her as the "saint like Hilda" and ardently wishes that she could remain "spotless" in the estimate of her "white-souled friend." Critics have also by and large attempted to perpetuate this view of Hilda, for example, Charles Feidelson who sees Hilda as a purely allegorical creature equipped with "white robe, tower, lamp and doves."[67] But in Hawthorne's world, a fatality "attaches to creatures too richly endowed." No one quite escapes evil or the taint of evil.

When Hilda sees Donatello kill the monk-shadow (at Miriam's instigation), she withdraws as completely as she can from basic human conditions. Hawthorne comments that it was "this unreality of the world" which made her so. But the more appropriate fact is that it is the reality and Hilda's inability to accept it, which makes her withdraw. She desires to keep Miriam away from her. She totally and irrevocably shuns her former friend. In her rejection of Miriam, Hilda has broken all ties with ordinary sinful humanity. Hilda is rigid in her stance. She does not seek to understand, only to withdraw:

> I do not understand, and may God keep me from understanding, how two things so totally unlike can be mistaken for one another; nor how two mortal foes, as Right and Wrong surely are, can work together in the same deed. This is my faith; and I should be led astray, if you could persuade me to give it up.[68]

She is thus "falsely true." She cannot reconcile Good and Evil, unlike Kenyon. While Hilda breaks off all contact with Miriam after the murder, Kenyon pursues Donatello and is sympathetic towards him. However, his growing love for Hilda finally turns him away from the guilty lovers when they meet on the Campagna. He abjures contact, preferring a life of withdrawal like Hilda. He gives up his Miltonic justification of the fall. He turns to Hilda for guidance "forgive me, Hilda...O Hilda Guide me home." Hilda is a woman of "fugitive and cloistered virtue, unexercised and unbreathed, that never sallies out and sees her adversary, but sinks out of the race, where the immortal garland is to be run for, not without dust and heat."[69] Donatello and Miriam wander away to embark upon a life of repentance and expiation. Miriam's pilgrimage takes place at the Capuchin cemetery, a scene of shrines and tombs. As a penance, she gives the sacristan money "an amount that made his eyes open wide and glisten."[70] Donatello's pilgrimage takes place on the road back to Rome, when he stops at shrines along the way: "Beholding these consecrated stations, the idea seemed to strike Donatello of converting the otherwise aimless journey into a penitential pilgrimage."[71] The transformation that takes place in Miriam and Donatello is that they reach greater and deeper levels of understanding of the regenerative power of sin. When Miriam poses the question of the fortunate fall to Kenyon, that sin may be the necessary means of salvation, he is aghast at the assumption: "It is too dangerous Miriam! I cannot follow you.... Mortal man has no right to tread on the ground where now you set your feet."[72] The end of the novel sees Hilda and Kenyon as a happy married couple. Kenyon who abdicated "truth" in favour of Hilda's "orthodoxy" will no longer be a "consummate artist" but a respectable carver of button holes. Unlike Hilda and Kenyon, Donatello and Miriam have looked deeply into human nature. They gain insight at the cost of happiness.

In linking the fall myth to human destinies, Hawthorne shows profound insight into man and a compassionate understanding of his plight. The problem of good and evil is complex and admits of no one solution. The borderline between good and evil is a narrow one. Evil resulting in much that is good as in the case of Miriam and Donatello, and Good producing the evil of isolated intellects as in the case of Hilda. In Hawthorne, "There is no synthesis...only thesis and antithesis in balance."[73]

End Notes

1. *Literary History of America* (New York, 1900), 433.
2. Cited by F.O. Matthuessen, *American Renaissance* (New York, 1941), 193.

3. Nina Baym, *The Scarlet Letter: A Reading* (Boston: Twaynes Publishers, 1986), Chap-3, 52-82.
4. Nathaniel Hawthorne, *Complete Works*, IX, 43.
5. *Ibid.*, 20-21.
6. A. Robert Lee, *Nathaniel Hawthorne: New Critical Essays* (London: Vision Press Ltd., 1982), 187-228.
7. D. Deleuze and F. Guattari, *Anti-Oedipus* (New York: Viking Press, 1977), 256.
8. *The Scarlet Letter: A Reading*, 52-82.
9. Nathaniel Hawthorne, *The Scarlet Letter*, 89.
10. *Ibid.*, 164.
11. Iric Mottram, *Power and Law in Hawthorne's Fiction*, 197.
12. *The Scarlet Letter* (New York: Oxford University Press, 1962), 256 (All references are to this edition).
13. *Ibid.*, 256.
14. *Ibid.*, 67. 15. *Ibid.*, 144.
16. *Ibid.*, 145-46.
17. *Ibid.*, 145-46.
18. *Ibid.*, 76. 19. *Ibid.*, 171. 20. *Ibid.*, 252.
21. *Ibid.*, 172-173.
22. *Ibid.*, 243.
23. Eric Mottram, *Power and Law in Hawthorne's Fiction*, 191.
24. *The Scarlet Letter*, 102.
25. *Ibid.*, 91.
26. *Ibid.*, 91.
27. *Ibid.*, 256.
28. Nathaniel Hawthorne, *Complete Works*, VI, 208.
29. Richard Harter Fogle, *Hawthorne's Fiction: The Light and the Dark* (Norman: University of Oklahama Press, 1952), 150 (All references are to this edition).
30. J.A. Leo Lemay, ed., *The American Reader* (Washington DC: United States Information Agency, 1938), 277.
31. Nathaniel Hawthorne, *The House of the Seven Gables*, 2.
32. *Ibid.*, 3.
33. *Hawthorne's Fiction: The Light and the Dark*, 155.
34. *The House of the Seven Gables*, 1.
35. *Ibid.*, 251.

36. *Ibid.*, 309.
37. *Ibid.*, 81.
38. *Ibid.*, 16.
39. *Ibid.*, 19-20.
40. *Hawthorne's Fiction*: *The Light and the Dark*, 153.
41. *The House of the Seven Gables*, 14.
42. George Norlin, *The Quest of American Life* (Boulder Co.: University of Colorado Press, 1945), xi.
43. O.B. Frothingham, *Transcendentalism in New England*: *A History* (New York: Putnam, 1876), 105-06.
44. Mason Wade, ed., *Writings of Margaret Fuller* (New York: Viking Press, 1941), 150.
45. Henry James, *Hawthorne* (New York: Harper and Brothers, 1879), 133.
46. *The Complete Works of Nathaniel Hawthorne* (Boston, 1896), 14 (All subsequent references are to this edition).
47. *Ibid.*, 4, 192
48. *Ibid.*, 68.
49. *Ibid.*, 170.
50. *Ibid.*, 170.
51. *Ibid.*, 223-24.
52. *The Prophetic Pictures*, 178.
53. Roy R. Male, *Hawthorne's Tragic Vision* (New York: Norton Library, 1964), 151.
54. *Blithedale Romance*, 28.
55. Darrel Abel, *The Moral Picturesque*: *Studies in Hawthorne's Fiction* (Indiana: Purdue University Press, 1988), 285.
56. *Blithedale Romance*, 122-23.
57. Emerson, "New England Reformers", *Works,* 261.
58. *Blithedale Romance*, 218.
59. *Ibid.*, 224.
60. Reprinted from *New England Quarterly,* XL (March, 1967), 61-78, by permission of the new England Quarterly and the author.
61. *The Marble Faun*, 370.
62. Darrel Abel, *The Moral Picturesque: Studies in Hawthorne's Fiction* (Indiana: Purdue University Press, 1988), 305.
63. *The Marble Faun,* 102.

64. *Ibid.*, 33.
65. *Ibid.*, 238.
66. Marius Gewley, *The Complex Fate* (London, 1952), 46.
67. Charles Feildelson, *Symbolism and American Literature* (Chicago, 1958), 15.
68. *The Marble Faun*, 437.
69. *Seventeenth Century Prose and Poetry*, 402.
70. *The Marble Faun*, 228.
71. *Ibid.*, 341 72. *Ibid.*, 840.
73. R.H. Fogle, *Hawthorne's Fiction*, 168.

For should Man finally be lost, should Man Thy creature late so lov'd, thy youngest Son fall circumvented thus by Fraud?....

So should thy Goodness and thy greatness both Be question'd and blasphem'd without defence.

"Paradise Lost"

—Milton

Part-II

Herman Melville confronts the problem of good and evil as did his colleague Nathaniel Hawthorne. In *Mardi and a Voyage Thither*, *Moby-Dick* or, *The White Whale* and *Pierre*, or *the Ambiguities*, Melville presents three aspects of man's intellectual and spiritual existence. Man is seen as a victim of truth, fate and virtue, respectively. Melville was obsessed with the eternal drama he saw within man: "We begin to live when we have conceived life as a tragedy." Melville admits to no resolution because life is not a struggle between good and evil, rather he saw corruption at the heart of good. Good and Evil were not antithetical but rather alike. Melville holds a mirror to Divine Depravity, so convincingly portrayed in *Billy Budd*.

Melville's works read as psychological probings into the subjective individual consciousness. The "I" in *Moby-Dick* is descriptive of the soul's voyage and includes a great many things seen and unseen. Ishmael is the intellectual observer, the only witness to Moby-Dick. His isolation mirrors Melville's isolation as also the loneliness of modern man. Rooted in disbelief, cut off from an inner world of certainty, all is doubtful, in eternal flux like the sea. Since man has lost his identity, like Adam, he has to wander in search of a lost paradise.

He has to find a connection between himself and the world around him. Picture Ishmael as looking into the inscrutable waters, seeking a meaning to existence. Melville placed a sharp focus in the feeling of "exile" or "abandonment" so common to modern man. In "Self and Experience", in the writings of Herman Melville, Merlin Bowen comments: "Running through all of Melville's work is the theme of banishment. Again and again in his writings we encounter the figure of the orphan, the outcast, the disinherited son."[1]

These two aspects, that man is on a quest and lives in self-proclaimed exile are endemic to the greatest works of Herman Melville. In *Mardi*, the quest is for truth with its corollary of happiness. Taji, the protagonist, is in search of the beautiful Yillah, who symbolizes, among other things, the pristine happiness of youth. Although *Mardi* begins with a blow-by-blow account of whaling, it soon drifts into a complex allegory. Taji's problems begin with the seizure of the maiden Yillah from the raft, followed by the landing at Odo and thereafter, her sudden disappearance. Truth and happiness are an interlude in the life of man. The plot from this point is purely allegorical and the characters have a symbolic dimension to them.

Babbalanja is the embodiment of reason, Yoomy of imagination, Media symbolises prudence, while Mohi is the repository of the transcendent quality of understanding. Taji is a one-dimensional character whose mono-maniacal desire is the recovery of Yillah. Having tasted happiness, man remains in search of the lost paradise. Taji shares alike the indomitable Will with Pierre and Ahab. Nothing daunts him, no obstacle put in his way alters him, not even the arrows of the avengers, which miss their mark. Taji avers allegiance to his course: "But I will not mind. And ever arrows follow, still will I hunt on."[2]

The attractions of the sensual temptress Hautia do not dissuade him. Nothing and no one can turn Taji away from the pursuit of Yillah—Truth: "Nor ever will I woo her, though she woo me till I die—Though Yillah never bless my eyes."[3] Commenting upon the single-mindedness of the Melvillian character, Bowen says:

> Mind and Will, already waked to action by the sting of his own experience, drive him on in pursuit of an answer. But ironically, this pursuit itself leads him ever farther away from the particular human ties and affections in whose interest it began. Repeated disappointments and humiliations breed a smouldering anger of a more personal sort until at last pity gives way to a monomaniac fury which sees nothing but the hated object.[4]

This conversely applies to Love too. The quest for love, truth and happiness is counterproductive and carries within it the seeds of destruction.

The quest for Yillah comes to naught in spite of having explored "The Golden Aztec Glades." Babbalanja is persuaded by the sheer weight of circumstances to accept a "lover, or at least shift his conceit of attainable felicity" and accept a sad tranquility. Reason thus accepts what Taji—the "Will" cannot. Taji's other companions, Media, Yoomy and Mohi, are more than inclined to follow Babbalanja. Taji alone remains unmoved by the Serenian Gospel of resignation. Babbalanja tries to dissuade Taji from a continued search in almost the same vein as Starbuck does Ahab in *Moby-Dick*.

Taji is, however, adamant in his resolve, "fixed as fate" and embarks upon the further search. Albeit unwillingly, all his companions except Babbalanja, follow him. Taji possesses the fustian quality which can never turn back:

> I am the hunter, that never rests! The hunter without a home! She I seek, still flies before, and I will follow, though she lead me beyond the reef, through sunless seas, and into might and death. Her, will I seek, through all the isles and stars; and find her, what're betide.[5]

In seeking after Yillah, Taji courts danger in the shape of Hautia, the dark enchantress. However, the quest for Yillah leads to nowhere. The futility of seeking to recapture a lost dream is all too apparent. Perhaps Taji realizes the fact; he had known it all along. Finally, with his mission unaccomplished and deserted by his companions, he seizes the helm himself and turns the prow out through the reef to the unplumbed depths beyond. His suicidal despair goads him to a point of no return. But even death or destruction is a self-appointed destination. The indomitable Will proclaims man's Sovereignty; his repudiation of the powers that be which deny his happiness:

> I am my own soul's emperor and my first act is abdication!
>
> Hail! realm of shades![6]

Taji's final act is one of Promethean pride and defiance. Although Taji possesses rudimentary character and is one dimensional yet we see in him the beginnings of the great Melvillian characters characterised by vigour, vitality and immense power, one who insisted upon an equal footing with the powers that be and a just appreciation of the sovereignty of Man. In a letter to his erstwhile friend Nathaniel Hawthorne, Melville emphasizes the fact that:

> The man who...declares himself a sovereign nature (in himself) amid the powers of heaven, hell and earth. He

> may perish, but so long as he exists he insists upon treating with all powers upon an equal basis. If any of these other powers choose to withhold certain secrets, let them; that does not impair my sovereignty in myself;
>
> That does not make me tributary.[7]

Mardi saw man in pursuit of truth or its corollary happiness which, in the ultimate analysis becomes counterproductive, even self-destructive.

Pierre sees man as a victim of virtue. Too much virtue becomes fatal. Herman Melville was to say of his conception of Pierre that:

> I am more frank with Pierre than the best men are with themselves. I am all unguarded and magnanimous with Pierre, therefore you see his weakness, and therefore only. In reverse men build imposing characters, not in revelations. He who shall be wholly honest, though nobler than Ethan Allen; that man shall stand in danger of the nearest mortal's scorn.[8]

Pierre's greatness lies in heroic defiance of the limitations of his own nature. There are two aspects to Pierre which get revealed as the story unfolds. He is the deluded romantic of the first half as well as the defiant rebel of the later half. In keeping with Melville's scrutiny of the evil in the heart of Good, *Pierre* reads as an initiation story, the account of a young man's introduction to life but the sinister implications being that it records the hero's growing awareness of his limitation rather than his powers, of his discovery that "the world offers not so much an open field for the exercise of his talents as an insuperable barrier to their realisation."[9] As always with Melville, there is a symbolic quality to Pierre. He begins as an untouched Adam of a modern Paradise. His shocked initiation into life begins when he realises that his father's "holier-than-thou" image is wholly tarnished by revelations about his indiscretions. Pierre Glendinning, a young man of promise is betrothed to Lucy Tartar, whom he loves dearly. On the very day of fixing a date for his wedding, a letter is delivered to him telling him of a mysterious stranger who turns out to be Isabel Banford, his illegitimate half-sister.

The choice before Pierre is clear, either he exposes the infamy of his supposedly saintly father and his mother to shame or he keeps quiet and makes alternative arrangements for Isabel, which would secure her future without loss of family prestige. The real tragedy for Pierre is not in the choices he must make but in the fact that the moral fabric of his world has been torn asunder; reduced to "a charred Landscape within him." Beauty, delight, wealth prove to be mere gildings on "the base rivets and the chains of lies." Ugliness, Poverty and Infamy become the true "ministers of truth."

Herman Melville, like Hawthorne before him, was concerned with the problem of good and evil but for Melville, the problem of "iniquity" is never resolved. Pierre comes to the tragic realisation that more the heart is stirred by a noble cause, the closer does one come to the revelation of the falsity of the world:

> Such emotions as that Sermon raises in the enthusiastic hearts; such emotions all youthful hearts refuse to ascribe to humanity as their origin. This is of God! cries the heart, and in that cry ceases all inquisition. Now, with the fresh-read Lermon in his soul, the youth again gazes abroad upon the World. Instantly...an overpowering sense of the world's downright positive falsity comes over him: the world seems to lie saturated and soaking with lies....[10]

The disillusionment of Pierre further reveals the unchristian harshness of his mother to Delly Ulves, the fallen village girl and even to Pierre himself. In his pursuit of virtue, Pierre makes the ultimate sacrifice of Lucy, of the woman he loves and that part of himself that loves her. He does this out of a mistaken notion of honour and loyalty. "Lively dedicated as he felt himself to be with divine commands upon him to befriend and champion Isabel, through all conceivable contingencies of Time and Chances, how could he insure himself against the insidious inroads of self-interest and hold intact all his unselfish magnanimities, if once he should permit the distracting thought of Lucy to dispute with Isabel's, the pervading possession of his soul."[11] Pierre, upon learning of his father's perfidy had rejected his illusions as a great falsity. Unfortunately, he fails to realise that although

Lucy is a part of his world, she is not false. Thus, Pierre's grief is twice as large, given the double sacrifice of his value system and of his love. In order to acknowledge the outcast Isabel publicly and give her her due, he breaks off with Lucy and enters into a counterfeit marriage with Isabel. Pierre thus unwittingly becomes involved in a web of deception. Lucy's agony at his behaviour disturbs him:

> Can then my conduct be right? Lo! by my conduct I seem threatened by the possibility of a sin anomalous and accused, so anomalous, it may well be the one for which Scripture says, there is never forgiveness. Corpses behind me, and that last sin before, how then can my conduct be right?[12]

Pierre feels that he has compounded his father's error with another and yet another. Financially he is faced with bankruptcy when Glen Stanley, who has become the heir to the Glendinning fortune, disowns him.

Financial ruin comes on the heels of moral perdition when Pierre recognises the fact that his altruistic feelings towards Isabel border on incest. The very Virtue he was seeking to protect is now threatened. In despair he questions the very foundation of virtue and vice: "Look: a nothing is the substance, it casts one shadow one way, and another the other way; and these two shadows cast from one nothing; these, seems to me, are Virtue and Vice."[13]

If Virtue and Vice are derived from nothing, they still threaten the happiness of man because of the psychological hold they have on man—"It is the law." The irony of man's position is that he can neither achieve Virtue nor renounce it. His earthly nature puts perfection beyond his reach, and his Godlike nature forever urges him towards it. Man is caught in a cleft stick. Pierre's tragedy is aggravated by the death of his mother. He sinks deeper and deeper into despair. He gives up all pretence of brotherly interest in Isabel. As he had repudiated the moral world, having discovered his father's duplicity even then, he is forced to discredit accountability when he discovers his own besmirched self. The threat of evil without had driven him only to a revelation of evil within: "I catch glimpses, and seem to half see, somehow, that the uttermost ideal of moral perfection in man is wide of the mark. The demi-God's temple on trash, and Virtue and Vice are trash! Isabel."[14]

The return of the lovely Lucy Tartar to his world with the noble intention of serving him to the very end provides no salve to his wounds. Even dry sterile intellectualism has denied him and he makes no progress with his book. Pierre is torn between Lucy and Isabel and he is driven to the point of no return. He begins to feel that he is a victim of a remorseless fate. The pursuit of truth and virtue has ended in an abject failure. Though doomed, Pierre will never give in. Merlin Bowen comments: "broadly understood, Titanism may be defined as an attitude of uncompromising resistance to a tyrannical and resistless power."[15] Pierre begins to see the sinister pattern inherent in the life:

> Now he began to feel that in him, the thaws of a Titan were forestallingly cut by the scissors of Fate…All things… seemed as created to mock and torment him. He seemed gifted with Loftiness, merely that it might be dragged down to the mud, still, the profound willfulness in him would not give up. Against the breaking heart, and the bursting head,...still he like a demi-God bore up. His soul's ship foresaw the inevitable rocks, but resolved to sail on, and make a courageous wreck.[16]

Pierre realizes that he has lost the game, deserted alike by the world and his own conscience, there is no turning back. Like Enceladus, nothing is left of him but his own maimed and armless trunk and this he hurls in a last defiant act at the hostile world and the indifferent Gods, destroying like Ahab, himself and those he loves.

In *Mardi* and *Pierre*, Melville shows man's abortive quest for virtue and truth. Further, when man digs into the moral fabric of existence all he finds is the bedrock of falsity and lies. Thus corruption is at the heart of Good. Both Taji and Pierre begin with a moral conscience which ultimately destroys them. They begin subservient to the moral code, which they unwittingly break and which forces them to ultimate rebellion. This code, or law, of conscience proves remorseless. Ahab belongs to a different category altogether. He begins where his predecessors left off. The rebel without a cause, the universal nothingness, which drives him to blind fury.

Henry A. Murray in "In Nomine Diaboli" comments: "Captain Ahab is an embodiment of that fallen angel or demi-God who in Christendom was variously named Lucifer, Devil, Adversary, Satan. The Church fathers would have called Ahab "Anti Christ" because he was not Satan himself, but a human creature possessed of all Satan's pride and energy, summing up within himself as Irenecus said, "the apostasy of the devil."[17] *Moby-Dick*, perhaps Melville's greatest, certainly his most characteristic work, bears varied interpretation. Taken from a Freudian standpoint, the whole represents Melville's puritan conscience against which his Ego or Ahab is engaged in a life and death struggle. Then again, Ahab has been described as a modern Christ or Prometheus resisting the evils of the white whale. On a more basic level, what *Moby-Dick* promises is a psychological analysis of man, who proclaims his sovereignty amidst the powers of Heaven or Hell, as the case may be. Ahab thus commits the Faustian blunder of considering himself superior to mankind. Ahab is aware of the fact that there are limitations to man's intellectual prowess, but instead of submitting to his weakness, he hopes to transcend it through sheer defiance. Much of *Moby-Dick* is given over to powerful allegory and symbol. Ishmael thus represents man's philosophical wanderings. His alter ego Ahab seeks to dominate nature (the white whale) and inflict his will upon it. Ahab thus seeks to destroy the white whale, which is symbolic of a "mono-maniac incarnation" of a superior power. He seeks to strip the mask off the face of nature, "If man will strike, strike through the mask! How can the prisoner react outside except by thrusting through the Wall." This is Ahab's quest and perhaps a universal one. Ahab faces a formidable opponent. The White Whale seems emblematic of two qualities. Firstly there is the visible aspect of life which seems forged out of love, and then there is the invisible aspect bordered with fear. It is this which man cannot face. Man is aware of his own nothingness in the face of Nature. His greatest fear being that he is an accident of Nature. Ahab, perhaps more than most men, feels the futility in the face of blind impersonal nature. He dreads the fact that there is "Naught, beyond."

His bitterness, in the face of uncertainty, mirrors what Freud underlined as a major problem of Modern Man. At an ethical level, perhaps Ahab sins against God and Man, but he was no fiend. Merely a man capable of storming the very gates of heaven—that inhuman silent world in order to reassert and reassure man of his place in Nature and give him back his feeling of relatedness, of which he has been dispossessed. But it is a losing battle as is amply qualified in *Moby-Dick*.

The plot of *Moby-Dick* is clear enough. Ishmael with his savage companion, Queequeg, joins the whaling ship Pequod at Nantucket, heading for the South Pacific. Before doing so, they happen to listen to Father Mapple's sermon on Jonah, which highlights man's perverse disobedience of God's commandments and its fateful consequences. Maurice Friedman comments:

> Father Maple's image of man is actually not Biblical but Calvinist. In contrast to the Boot of Jonah, his sermon is founded on a stern, transcendent God, a sinful world, and the moral duty of self-denial. This is the God the Gnostics and Doctor Faustus call the redeems God, and it really is the world of the Gnostics and Doctor Faustus rather than the world of the Hebrew Bible that we see here. The basic contrast here is between the dark wrath below and the redemption above.[18]

Ahab is basically a modern man confronted with a terrifying vision of reality which forces him below the surface and grapples with the ultimate concepts of Good and Evil. In order to arrive at truth, man must in a sense destroy God and begin at square one. Ahab is thus not unlike Dostoevsky's *Kirlov*, Nietzsche's *Superman*, or Sartre's *Orestes*. Man is driven to question God in his quest for existence. Unable to meet his creator in a one-to-one relation of equality, he is forced to assume the mantle of sin and depravity. Thus, in affirming God, he must deny himself. Father Mapple's sermon amply qualifies this idea, "This shipmates, this is that other lesson, and woe to the pilot of the living God who slights....Woe to him who seeks to pour oil upon the waters when God has brewed them into a gale!"[19] Man appears to be a dumb witness incapable of independent thought and action. His is not the reason "why."

Ahab, unlike Father Mapple's Jonah, affirms himself all good is identified with the self; all evil with that which opposes the self. The shift of focus is all too apparent. Instead of God, man becomes the final arbiter of all things. In the chapter entitled "The Quarter—Deck" (XXXVI), the true purpose of the Voyage is revealed. Ahab is out to destroy Moby Dick, the White Whale. The sinister overtone is further heightened with Ahab rousing the men, the performance of the Black Mass in which the harpooners drib with their inverted harpoons. The only man who opposes Ahab is Starbuck, who finds its sheer madness, "Vengeance on a dumb brute!" Starbuck finds the entire tirade blasphemous—after all, the dumb brute was part of the natural world, a creation of God and therefore essentially good. Although the Whale is dangerous to man, Starbuck does not see any malice involved or intended to man.

Ahab, with an essentially Platonistic vision, delves below the "Mask" of reality, "The little lower layer"—which is both inscrutable and malicious. Below the beautiful and the mundane upper level is an inhuman, impersonal and anti-human reality. Man confronted with this hostile mass has one option—to strike at it:

> If man will strike, strike through the mask! How can the prisoner reach outside except by thrusting through the wall? To me, the white whale is that Wall, shoved near to me. Sometimes I think there's naught beyond. But 'tis enough. He tasks me: he heaps me; I see in him outrageous strength, with an inscrutable malice sinewing it.[20]

Ahab feels exonerated and justified in his actions. It is the natural scheme of things which compels this response. "I'd strike the sun if it insulted me. For could the sun do that, then could I do the other." (167). Thus in the face of a basically inscrutable reality, the only way man can find any meaning in his existence is to identify truth with himself and then attack reality that appears fair and beautiful but is really hostile and malignant to man. Thus Ahab's quest is universalized, and he manages to win over his crew to his quest. Even Ishmael feels the tug: "My shouts have gone up with the rest, my oath has been welded with theirs. A wild, mystical sympathetical feeling was in me; Ahab's quenchless feud seemed mine." (180). The White Whale, the object of Ahab's quest and hatred was a Sperm Whale of gigantic proportions, great ferocity and cunning. Above all, there is an element of the supernatural associated with it. To Ahab, it does not appear like an "unintelligent Agent." In *Moby-Dick,* Ishmael relives the fury of the White Whale: "Judge, then, to what pitches of inflamed, distracted fury the minds of his more desperate hunters were impelled, when amid the chips of chewed boats, and the sinking limbs of torn comrades, they swam out of the white curds of the Whale's direful wrath into the serene, exasperating sunlight that smiled on, as if at a birth or a bridal."[21] Ahab sees the horror not only in the maiming and death itself but the stark contrast between the reality which confronts Ahab and it leaves him with only one option: either go down submitting or go down defying. Moby-Dick represents metaphysical evil and Ahab, the whole of humanity. The crew of the Pequod likewise constitute a microcosm, with the sensible Starbuck as first mate, the easy-going Stubb as second mate, Flask as third mate and the harpooners Queequeg, Tashtego and Daggoo the Negro savage.

Although representative of humanity, Ahab stands hands and shoulders above his crew, set apart by two physical deformities, his ivory leg and a scar that runs the length of his body. More important are the psychic scars he bears, the signs of inner anguish, "a crucifiction in his face." He looks as if he has been cut away from the stake. Though inwardly tortured , he leaves no doubt about his innate superiority over all mankind.

Ahab's fight is every man's fight against the malignancy of Nature and above all its distortion and deformity as the whiteness of the whale suggests:

> What is it that the Albino man so peculiarly repels and often shocks the eye, as that sometimes he is loathed by his own kith and kin! It is that whiteness which invests him, a

> thing expressed by the name he bears. The albino is as well made as other men—has no substantive deformity—and yet this mere aspect of all-pervading whiteness makes him more strangely hideous than the ugliest abortion.[22]

Apart from its malignancy and deformity, another dreaded aspect of Nature is its Vulturism. In "The Funeral", this is amply qualified, "Oh, horrible Vulturism of death! From which the mightiest whale is not free." (300). Ahab is determined to part ways with Nature in every way. In "The Quadrant" (CXVII), Ahab tramples upon his quadrant, saying that if God had meant man to look upward, he could not have put our eyes level with the horizon. Ahab even dissociates with science, a form of co-operation with Nature whereby man received his greatest skills. To Ahab, Nature alone has the last world. In "Brit" (LVIII) Ishmael underlines: "...however baby man may brag of his science and skill, and however much, in a flattering future that science and skill may augment, yet forever and forever, to the crack of doom, the sea will insult and murder him and pulverize the Stateliest, Stiffest frigate he can make...".[23] The fury of nature and its representative Moby-Dick do not deter the mono-maniac pursuit of Ahab. The Pequod cruises for several weeks on the Atlantic and meets nine whaling, each of which is symbolically named the "Albatross", the "Town-Ho", the "Jeroboam", the "Rosebud", the "Samuel Enderby" of London. The Captain of the Samuel Enderby has not only seen Moby-Dick but has lost an arm to the white whale and staunchly abjures the prospect of further contact with the monstrous whale. This does not deter Ahab but rather whets his appetite.

Melville's Ahab, like Prometheus, defies nature in the hope of wresting out its secret, its inaccessible alter self. However, in the process of hunting out impersonal nature, Ahab begins to lose out on his human qualities. Even his unexpected affection for Pip who had been driven insane by fright (A causality of impersonal nature), Starbuck's attempts in "The Chase" to deter Ahab fall on deaf ears. Ahab feels fated to follow out his course, "The path to my fixed purpose is laid with iron rails, whereon my soul is groomed to run."[24] The three days of attack on Moby-Dick proves graphic reading. F.O. Matthiessen, in

American Renaissance (1941), calls Melville's account of the three days of the actual chase of Moby-Dick "the finest piece of dramatic writing in American literature."[25] The first day ends with Moby-Dick smashing the whaleboat. On the second day, Fedallah (Ahab's evil genius) disappears, and his whalebone leg is broken. On the final day of the chase, Fedallah's body reappears fastened by twisted lines to the body of the whale. Fedallah had predicted that Ahab's death would follow his own. On the third day, Ahab harpoons the white whale but is dragged to his death by the hamper rope (as predicted). In an ultimate symbol of the destructive powers of Nature, the white whale rams into the Pequod (the microcosm) and sinks it completely. Only Ishmael escapes floating upon Queequeg's coffin to tell the tale of the ill-fated ship. Thus, the voyage ends in total destruction, in the "total Wreck" that Ahab prefers to submit to human fate.

The archetypal myths of Prometheus and Faust have inevitably shown man's destruction in the hands of Nature. Not only is he destroyed but en route, some part of humanity is lost. A more modern-day analogy would be Kurtz in Joseph Conrad's *Heart of Darkness* or the children in William Golding's *Lord of the Flies*. In his pursuit of Nature, Melville's Ahab likewise takes on a demonic quality. In the chapter "Ahab and the Carpenter", Ahab talks of Prometheus fashioning men and speaks of his personal ideal:

> Hold: While Prometheus is about it, I'll order a complete man after a desirable pattern. Imprimis, fifty feet high in his socks; then, chest modelled after the Thames Tunnel; then, legs with roots to 'em, to stay in one place; then, arms three feet through the vorist; no heart at all, brass forehead, and about a quarter of an acre of fine brains; and let me see— shall I order eyes to see outwards? No, but put a sky- light on top of his head to illuminate inwards...[26]

This monolithic man-machine seems capable of withstanding any or all the destructive forces of Nature. Characteristically, this man mountain does not have a heart, the Achilles' heel of all human intercourse. Further, the eyes of this Creature are turned inward, illumined and illuminating the self, unlike the average man whose eyes are turned outward towards Nature.

In *Moby-Dick,* Melville delves into the mystery of ingenuity by locating his main protagonist in the familiar conflict of good and evil. Unfortunately, man faces his adversary, Nature and is mauled, mutilated and destroyed by his foe. As it is clearly evident in the early works, *Mardi*, *Pierre* and finally, in *Moby-Dick,* man fights a losing battle against the world, and any form of defiance only brings retribution. Having toyed with the idea of man and the powers that be, Melville considered a twist in the plot. Thus, in *Billy Budd,* instead of a defiant Ahab, we have a submissive Billy Budd, the epitome of goodness and virtue.

Critics have called *Billy Budd* Melville's "testament of acceptance." While E.L.G. Watson does not qualify the statement but looks at the story from his own angle. He is of the view that Melville was no longer a rebel and has come to accept evil. He no longer condemns its existence. Freeman likewise felt that Melville is at last resigned to the recognition of necessity; F.O. Matthiessen asserts that Melville had come to accept the existence of good and evil; Willard Thorp states that Melville calls for a truce.

However, there is another angle to be considered. Critics like Alfred Kazin, Richard Chase and Lawrence Thompson are dissatisfied with the testament of acceptance. Their interpretation, as well as those of Mumford, Weir, Sedgewick, Joseph Schiffman, Gay Wilson Allen, point to *Billy Budd* as a work of irony, bitter sarcasm even. An in-depth analysis of *Billy Budd* itself would prove that even if *Billy Budd* is a testament of acceptance, surely what is implied is not an acceptance of evil and the natural Goodness of God but rather an acceptance of evil and the divine depravity of God. In Milton's *Paradise Lost,* Man, the beloved son of God, is "circumvented by fraud" and thus "falls". In the final analysis, even the goodness and greatness of God can be questioned and blasphemed without defence. Herman Melville delves into the reasons behind the loss of faith and the hiatus between man and God. In this, he was not alone as Voltaire, Thomas Paine and Rousseau rejected alike the Calvinistic belief in the depravity of man and the concept of Original Sin. They argued that sin originated as did the Word of God. Thus, if man sinned, then it was God who caused him to do so. Thus, they replaced the concept of mortal sin with that of divine depravity. William York Tindall in his essay "The form of Billy Budd" comments: "By aid of myth and military ritual, the story of Billy, transformed from an essay on good, evil and choice, approaches what Yeats called "the ceremony of innocence..."[27] The story line of *Billy Budd* is clear enough. Billy Budd, a sailor, is symbolic of everything innocent. As his name suggests, he is a budlike man, having much in common with Carlyle's Hero in *Candide*. The evils of impressions find in Billy Budd, an easy prey when Captain Vere insists on him enlisting on board the "Indomitable" leaving the parent ship "Rights of Man." The names of the ships symbolically represent Calvinism on the one hand and on the other, the humane philosophy of Voltaire, Rousseau, Schopenhauer and Thomas Paine who insisted upon the Rights of Man over tyranny, the autocracy of Government, Religion or even God.

Billy Budd, as he appears at the beginning of the novel, is in a state of innocence. He is a second Adam or a prelapsarian Adam. Endowed with a trusting nature, he is unaware of evil, his handsome face is seconded by his handsome nature. William Braswell underlines the symbolic quality of the novel with the observation that:

> With the Indomitable, a microcosm representing Melville, certain aspects of his being are dramatised in Captain Vere, Billy Budd and Claggart. The divine or semi divine, origin of Melville's being is suggested in the fact that Vere is of noble lineage and that Billy and Claggart, although their origin is uncertain, are reputed to have nobleman's blood in their veins. The king is a symbol of the Deity: he does not physically appear in the story, but he is the supreme authority under whose law the ship operates.[28]

Billy Budd is a symbolic novel. As a symbol of all that is good, his impact upon the crew of the "Indomitable" is immediate. He wins the esteem of the "intelligent" section of the crew and the "tolerant Sarcasm" of the meaner members of the crew. *Billy Budd* abounds with the Adamic myth. If Billy is Adam, then Captain Vere is symbolic of God, a supposedly just equitable God.

Captain Vere is, above all, fair-minded with an eye for justice. The Edenesque myth is carried further by the personification of Evil or Satan alias Claggart, an officer on board the ship.

Melville takes pain to point out the fact that Claggart's evil, his malice, is not a product of environment or education or missed opportunity but is one of "natural depravity." The term "natural" implying God "ordained" depravity. Billy Budd or Adam has an Achilles' heel wherein he loses his voice under circumstances of stress. The analogy is very clear. Mere goodness is not effective in the face of a hostile world. This defect, in the otherwise perfect Billy Budd is like Claggart's evil, "God- given," not endemic to man. This shortcoming in Billy Budd proves fatal. Ethically it would imply that man is made imperfect by God and then "damned" by that imperfection.

Claggart's hatred for Billy Budd stems from his envy of Billy Budd's popularity and his innate contentment, which is a direct result of his state of innocence (Adam before the fall). This rouses Claggart's contempt as also his malice. In an attempt to destroy Billy Budd, Claggart implicates him in a plot to mutiny and denounces him to Captain Vere. Captain Vere, the just and good Captain of the ship mistrusts Claggart and is instinctively convinced of Billy Budd's innocence and Claggart's evil nature. In an attempt to arrive at the truth, Captain Vere decides to make Claggart denounce Billy Budd to his face. Captain Vere is certain that, given this situation, Billy Budd would retaliate by giving out his version of the story, thereby proving his innocence. Unfortunately, Billy Budd is so dumbfounded by the enormity of the accusation that he loses his voice temporarily. Symbolically it would imply that a natural or God-given defect betrays him at the very moment it is most required. Further, in the scheme of things, Goodness in the face of evil is inarticulate. Captain Vere realising Billy's predicament, reassures him by telling him to take his own time.

The unfortunate result of this deliberation upon Billy is that he is unable to use his tongue, his arm "shot out", and Claggart falls to the ground senseless. The true nature of Captain Vere is revealed in the manner in which he deals with the crime. Adam has sinned, Billy Budd has killed a superior officer aboard the "Indomitable." The penalty for such a crime is death. Captain Vere acts the part of witness, judge and jury. His assessment is equivocal. An officer has been killed and the penalty is death. He is aware that Billy Budd's actions were not deliberate. He was merely denouncing a liar. He had broken no natural law, only a man-made law. Besides, there was no malice involved nor any injury meant. As Billy Budd confesses in his trial:

> No, there was no malice between us. I never bore malice against the Master-at-arms. I am sorry he is dead. I did not mean to kill him. Could I have used my tongue I would not have struck him. But he foully lied to my face and in presence of my Captain and I had to say something and I could only say it with a blow, God help me![29]

Captain Vere, an epitome of blind justice deliberately chooses a jury who would be guided in their judgement by him. Billy Budd is pronounced guilty and sentenced to death.

E.L. Grant Watson, in his perceptive essay "Billy Budd as Testament", comments: "In Captain Vere we find a figure which may interestingly be compared to Pontius Pilate. Like Pilate, he condemns the just man to a shameful death knowing him to be innocent, but, unlike Pilate, he does not wash his hands, but manfully assumes full responsibility, and in such a way as to take the half, if not more than half of the bitterness of the execution upon himself."[30] Billy Budd is pronounced guilty and sentenced to death. The divine depravity which Melville so subtly suggests is all too evident. It was Captain Vere's puerile plot of forcing a showdown between Claggart and Billy Budd, which makes him confront Billy Budd leading to the subsequent action. In a sense, Captain Vere is directly responsible for the situation in which Billy Budd finds himself. God having created man as a lesser being susceptible to temptation, the original sin, consequently punishes him for having sinned. Even so, Captain Vere is responsible for Billy Budd's fate. William Braswell, speaking of the relationship between the two, says, "The relationship between the two, suggestive as it is of the relationship between Abraham and Isaac, and between God the Father and the Son, apparently enables Billy to understand that Vere's role is necessitated by his adherence to forms which he holds dearer than life itself...."[31] In keeping with his pristine innocence Billy Budd submits to his father figure Captain Vere's interpretation of his crime.

But Billy Budd is innocent. The Chaplain who visits him to prepare him for death is overwhelmed by a human affection for him. He realises that Budd possesses a peace greater than any he can prepare him for. Critics have identified Captain Vere with Pontius Pilate, who condemns an innocent Christ to the cross. However, there is no turning back. Captain Vere is blinded by his sense of justice which he follows to the letter, entirely ignoring the spirit behind it, that is, overlooking the mitigating circumstances which initiated the crime. A law had been infringed—punishment must follow. In keeping with the provisions of the Law of Moses and entirely overlooking Christ's gentle version of justice tempered with mercy.

In keeping with the dark justice, Billy Budd must die. But that his death must be taken as yet another crucifixion is amply clear. His fellow sailors intuitively and instinctively realise that he is innocent of the charge of murder and mutiny. He dies a martyr's death: an innocent sacrifice at the altar of an "Angry God" to use the phraseology of Jonathan Edwards "this image of mankind as sinners in the hands of an Angry God."

In his final novel, Melville makes it amply clear that the "problem of iniquity" is never resolved. Man could seek out an ideal as in *Mardi* or *Billy Budd*. But the fact remains that it all comes to nought in the face of Divine Depravity, which has planted the fatal flaw in man, then destroys him for owning up to it. Hawthorne's characters regain a semblance of Paradise or at least peace, albeit at a personal cost. Melville's characters merely hurl defiance at the face of Heaven or Hell as the case may be or submit to die. Thus, both Hawthorne and Melville saw man at odds with the world, whether it was the evils of Puritanism or Calvinism he was fighting. Man stands alone, a lesser Prometheus, alienated alike from God and the world. Thus, unlike Emerson, Thoreau and Whitman, the characters of Hawthorne and Melville do not really achieve the requisite blend of egoistic and altruistic motivations in the Self.

End Notes

1. Merlin Bowen, *Self and Experience in the Writings of Herman Melville* (Chicago: The University of Chicago Press, 1960), 128-97.
2. Herman Melville, *Mardi*, I (Chap. C), 356-58.
3. *Ibid.*, I (Chap. CI), 359.
4. Merlin Bowen, *Self and Experience in the Writings of Herman Melville*, 128-97.
5. *Mardi* (Chap. CLXXXIX), 380-82.
6. *Ibid.* (Chap. CXCV), 399-400.
7. R.K. Gupta, ed., *Essays of American Literature* (Hyderabad: ASRC), 81.
8. Herman Melville, *Pierre* (Book V, Chap. vii), 151-52.
9. Merlin Bowen, *Defiance: The Way of Tragic Heroism*, 158-59.
10. *Pierre* (Book XIV, Chap. II), 289-90.
11. *Ibid.* (Book V, Chap. V), 148-49.
12. *Ibid.* (Book XIV, Chap. I), 285-88.
13. *Ibid.* (Book XIX, Chap. II), 381-82.
14. *Ibid.*
15. Merlin Bowen, *Self and Experience in the Writings of Herman Melville*, 128-197.
16. Herman Melville, *Pierre* (Book XXIII, Chap. IV), 443.
17. Henry A. Murray, *The New England Quarterly*, XXIV, 435-52 (December, 1951).
18. Harold Bloom, ed., *Ahab* (New York: Chelsea House Publishers, 1991), 81-103.
19. Herman Melville, *Moby-Dick or The White Whale* (New Delhi: Eurasia Publishing House, 1966), 63.
20. *Ibid.*, 167.
21. *Ibid.*, 185.
22. *Ibid.*, 192.
23. *Ibid.*, 270.
24. *Ibid.*, 170-71.
25. F.O. Matthuessen, *American Renaissance* (New York: Oxford University Press, 1941), 421.
26. *Moby-Dick*, 445.
27. William, T. Stafford, *Melville's 'Billy Budd' and the Critics* (Belmont: Wadsworth Publishing House, 1961), 129.
28. *Ibid.*, 92.
29. Herman Melville, *Billy Budd*, 46-47.
30. *Melville's 'Billy Budd' and the Critics*, 76. 31. *Ibid.*, 100.

4

Walt Whitman: The Divine Average

One's-Self I sing, a simple separate person,

Yet utter the Word Democratic, the word En-Masse of Physiology from top to toe I Sing,

Not Physiognomy alone nor brain alone is worthy for the Muse, I say the Form complete is worthier far, The Female equally with the Male I sing.

Of life immense in passion, pulse, and power, Cheerful, for freest action form'd under laws divine, The modern man I sing.

"One's-Self I Sing"
—Walt Whitman

There is a certain ambiguity about Walt Whitman, the poet of *Leaves of Grass* (1855). Perhaps there are as many aspects to Whitman as there are interpretations of *Leaves of Grass*. This is because the text lends itself easily to analysis. In fact, it can be beaten into any shape.

Havelock Ellis, an early critic, links the morality of Whitman with that of Aristotle. To Van Wyck Brooks,[1] Whitman "precipitated the American character." Henry Alonzo Myers underlines Whitman's concept of spiritual democracy; Malcolm Cowley connects Walt Whitman's "Song of Myself" with Hindu mysticism; Karl Shapiro sees Whitman as a forerunner of D.H. Lawrence. Every nation on the globe has appropriated Whitman for its own, as is evident in Iwao Matsuhara's essay "Walt Whitman in Japan." There are critics like Bernice Slote who see Whitman as one more enduring link in the chain of life writers like D.H. Lawrence, Hart Crane and Dylan Thomas. Attempts have been made by critics like Lawrence Templin to trace the Quaker influence on Whitman. Besides, criticism of Whitman has not always been positive. Charges of pornography, perversion, inverted sexuality, and over-developed Oedipus complex notwithstanding, there are the likes of David Cavitch, who, in his chapter "The Frontiers of Sex", comes to a comprehensive understanding of the levels of sexuality in Whitman. Perhaps there is one quality in Whitman which has all too often been emphasized. This is his prophetic quality. David Daiches thus calls him the "Impressionist Prophet", while J. Middleton Murry hails him as the "Prophet of Democracy." Anthony Burgess underlines this fact: "There are passages of Whitman, as of Blake, which have a ring of something from the Apocrypha. This is appropriate for the age of the American Vision which produced him or which he—and President Lincoln and Mrs. Beecher Stowe—helped to produce."[2] It is as a prophet, a visionary and a seer that Whitman takes his place among the great humanistic writers of the 19th Century.

The fatalistic streak which was so much a part of Hawthorne and Melville is nowhere found in Walt Whitman. His was a glorious celebration—a prophetic awareness of man. *The Leaves of Grass* is an attempt to come to terms with himself and his visionary insights. His poems have an organic form, an integrity almost like the movements of a symphony. His avowed intention was to see that his "...poems when complete should be a unity, in the same sense that the earth is, or that the human body, (senses, soul, hand, trunk, feet, blood, viscera, man-root, eyes, hair), or that a perfect musical composition is..."[3]

The first movement in *Leaves of Grass* is towards "Selfhood." The 'self' is not merely the identity of a person or the sum total of his 'experiences.' The 'self' is the result of a true union between the body and the soul. Whitman toys with the idea of an initiation rite. The explicitly sexual overtones in section 5 of

"Song of Myself" can be read as a creativity myth—the union of body and soul, heaven and earth or male and female.

> I mind how once we lay such a transparent summer morning,
> How you settled your head athwart, my hips and turn'd over upon me,
> And parted the shirt from my bosom-bone, and plunged your tongue to my bare-strip heart,
> And reach'd till you felt my beard, and reach'd till you held my feet.
> Swiftly arose and spread around me the peace and knowledge that pass all the argument of the earth,
> And I know that the hand of God is the promise of my own,
> And I know that the spirit of God is the brother of my own,
> And that all the men ever born are also my brothers, and the women my sisters and lovers,
> And that a Kelson of the creation is love
> And limitless are leaves still or drooping in the fields
> And brown ants in the little wells beneath them,
> And mossy scabs of the worm fence, heap'd stones, elder, mullein and poke-weed.[4]

The emergent 'self' is not the limited empirical self, rather it is the universal self which embraces everything, the past, the present, the future, the old, the young, the good, the evil, everything that exists or existed through space and time. Thus, what we have in a nutshell is an embodiment of Schopenhauer's maxim—"the World is my idea." This was what Emerson had emphasized: "In all my lectures, I have taught one doctrine, namely the infinitude of the private man."[5] Thus, the unlimited 'self' is the first requirement of Whitman's prophetic vision of man.

The 'Self' so conceived adheres to the principle of equality. Equality or Democracy is not so much a political ideal as a Spiritual democracy. A major part of "Song of Myself" reads as a protest against a superficial classification of people as they appear in society. Thus, mechanics, labourers, runaway slaves, drunkards, thieves and prostitutes have an inner reality which partakes of infinitude and equality. Thus no occupation can limit the soul; no occupation can deprive it of participation in the inner world. The difference between the Madonna and Magdalene is, in essence, skin deep. This unwritten brotherhood of man in which the 'self' partakes makes a travesty of good and evil. All experiences are welcome to the 'self.' In "Starting from Paumanok" (section 7), Whitman clarifies:

> Omnes! Omnes! let others ignore what they may,
>
> I make the poem of evil also, I commemorate that part also,
>
> I am myself just as much evil as good, and my nation is and I say there is in fact no evil or if there is I say it is just as important to you, to the land or to me, as anything else.[6]

The 'Self' remains impassive, taking in all experiences, rejecting none:

> Me Imperturbe, standing at case in Nature
>
> Master of all or mistress of all, aplomb in the midst of irrational things,
>
> Imbued as they, passive, receptive, silent as they...[7]

Having established the fact that infinitude and equality are attributes of the 'Self', Whitman turns his attention to the puritan dichotomy of the body and soul. He realises that the "self" is basically integrated—that body and soul are one. There was nothing higher or lower, pristine or grass, God and the self were identical:

> I have said that the soul is not more than the body, And I have said the body is not more than the soul, And nothing, not God, is greater to one than one's self is...[8]

The visionary insights of Walt Whitman let him proclaim, "In the faces of men and women I see God, and in my own face in/the glass...."[9] This bold assertion led to a lot of negative criticism, and Whitman was much too often denounced as an egotist, a heretic, narcissist and the like. No doubt that there was an overriding optimism in Whitman, which made him push the concept of the "self" to its utmost limit. Although Whitman's metaphysics remained without a form; He followed his personal insights, which seemed to comprehend the past and the present, everything written or thought down the ages. He did not reject anything, rather his was a vast amalgamation:

> I do not despise you priests, all time, the world over, My faith is the greatest of faiths and the least of faiths,
>
> Enclosing worship ancient and modern and all between ancient and modern
>
> Believing I shall come again upon the earth after five thousand years
>
> Waiting responses from oracles, honouring the Gods, saluting the sun...[10]

Thus, having begun with a concern for the identity of the 'Self' and enunciated its attribute of equality and infinitude, Whitman proceeds with the initiation of the self into "Self-consciousness"—the great oneness, the experience of infinity, the triumph of the living spirit, which includes everything.

D.H. Lawrence, in his perceptive essay on Whitman, comments: "Whitman is drunk with the new wine of this new great experience, really drunk with the strange wine of infinitude....

It is man's maximum state of consciousness, his highest state of spiritual being. Supreme spiritual consciousness and the divine consciousness of supreme consciousness. It is reached through embracing love."[11]

Self-consciousness implies a union, a sexless union with the family, the nation, the race, and the world at large. The 'Self' participates in a pure process of assimilation. In "Autumn Rivulets", there is a poem called "There was a Child Went Forth" where Whitman qualifies this idea:

> There was a child went forth everyday,
>
> And the first object he looked upon, that object he became,

> And that object became part of him for the day or a certain part of the day or for many years or stretching cycles of years.[12]

The child and the object are integrated in a process of self-consciousness.

If the first movement of *Leaves of Grass* is the birth of the 'Self', the second movement of *Leaves of Grass* is towards the regenerative powers of the 'Self' expressed in sexual union. If the creativity myth forms the background to "Song of Myself" then the Adamic myth informs "Children of Adam." In "Children of Adam", Whitman challenges the Calvinistic belief in the depravity of man. The orthodox Christian concept of the innate evil in the heart of man and his resultant fall is re-interpreted. According to the Book of Genesis, Adam, through his disobedience (tempted by Eve) degraded his original innocence and brought death to the world. Having been conceived in sin and born of the flesh, subsequently, each man must qualify for a spiritual rebirth and thus regain paradise.

Walt Whitman inverts this ideal. It is not Adam but his "Children"—his descendants who have lost the garden through self-degradation. To regain paradise, man must purge not the physical but the sense of the physical as sinful. He must be born again not through a spiritual denial of the flesh but through the spiritual transfiguration of the flesh. Man should admit and glory in the Adamic or Sexual part of his nature. The resurrection of man is in his sexual body:

> To the garden the world a new ascending, Potent, mates, daughters, sons preluding,
>
> The love, the life of their bodies, meaning and the being,
>
> Curious here behold my resurrection after slumber.[13]

The Adamic man thus awakens to the life of the body— to the amorous, to the erotic and to phallic consciousness. The initiation into the life of the body has its ritualistic aspect. The Adamic man is immersed, cleansed, purified, and baptised in sex. In "I sing the body Electric", Whitman explicates:

> ....Bridegroom night of love working surely and softly into the prostrate dawn,

Undulating into the willing and yielding day,
Lost in the cleave of the clasping and sweet fleshe'd day,
This the nucleus—after the child is born of woman, man is born of woman,
This is the bath of birth, this the merge of small and large, and the outlet again.[14]

Paradoxically, it is through the sex experience, not by suppression of it, that man is reborn, that he is able to find his way back to the lost innocence of the garden of Eden. The first birth is that of the child, an outlet into life. But this implies imprisonment in the 'Self.' The second stage implies the rebirth through Sex to a "greater-than-self." Walt Whitman emphasized the fact that it was through a woman that the child receives its body at birth and it is through a woman that the man realizes his soul in rebirth. James E. Miller elaborates upon this aspect in Whitman by stating that "One is reminded of the mystical function of woman in the Christian tradition: The Virgin Mary, mother of Christ, or the Beatrice of Dante, or the 'Lady of Silence' of T.S. Eliot."[15] Thus, the Adamic man is an offshoot of the Adamic woman:

This is the female form
A divine number exhales from it from head to foot, It attracts with fierce undeniable attraction
I am drawn by its breath as if I were no more than a helpless
Vaper, all falls aside but myself and it...[16]

She is Eve and, in a literal and metaphoric sense, contains all. "A woman waits for me, she contains all, nothing is lacking/ yet all mere lacking if sex were lacking, or if the moisture of the right/man mere lacking."[17] The Adamic Woman contains all her descendants. This conceit of sex containing the immortality of the race is developed throughout the poem "A woman waits for me." It is only through the sexual act that the procession of life continues. The body which the Adamic man celebrates is not the mere body but the body "Electric:"

I sing the body electric
The armies of those I love engirth me and I engirth them

> They will not let me off till I go with them, respond to them
>
> And discorrupt them, and charge them full with the charge of the soul.[18]

The "electricity" referred to is the spiritual life of the body. People who have lost the instinct for life are like batteries that are lifeless. They must be "discorrupted"—recharged. The task of the Adamic man becomes doubly difficult because people would like to glorify the soul at the expense of the body.

All the poems in "Children of Adam" celebrate some aspect of the sexual experience. The body is roused to divinity and new life through phallic or pro-creative consciousness. The Adamic man is attracted to the woman by a strong magnetic attraction that will not be denied. Out of this vital union alone can the "Divine Average" the new man issue forth. If in the orthodox Christian Pantheon, Eve issued from the rib of Adam, the new Adamic race has to be "Unfolded" out of a woman. This idea is central to the poem "Unfolded out of folds", which forms a part of "Autumn Rivulets."

> Unfolded out of the folds of the woman man comes unfolded, and is always to come unfolded
>
> Unfolded only out of the superbest women of earth is to come the superbest man of the earth...[19]

This emphasis on rebirth through sex was not intrinsic to Whitman alone. D.H. Lawrence, in *Fantasia of the Unconscious*, comes to a like conclusion. In the chapter on "The Birth of Sex," Lawrence parallels Whitman: "But what is experience? Untellable. Only, we know something, we know that in the act of coition, the blood of the individual man, acutely surcharged with intense vital electricity—we know no word to say "electricity by analogy—rises to a culmination, in a tremendous magnetic urge towards the magnetic blood of the female. The whole of the living blood in the two individuals forms a field of intense, polarised magnetic attraction. A great flash of interchange occurs, like an electric spark when two currents meet or like lightening out of the densely charged clouds."[20] Whitman's "body electric" likewise is not merely a sensual body—but a body that is primitive, natural and innocent which cleaves to the woman. The Adamic spirit is always present when a man indulges in a physical action unselfconsciously without shame. The brief but vivid vignettes of people performing simple activities—the child at the mother's breast, the swimmers in all their nakedness, the apprentice boys wrestling confirm this spirit.

This brings us to the third movement in *Leaves of Grass,* which is towards camaraderie. Whitman, like Lawrence after him, was acutely concerned with human relationships beyond the procreative man-woman union. The "Calamus" aspect of *Leaves of Grass* dramatises the intensely passionate individual attachment and camaraderie which forms the basis of true democracy. Thus the "Calamus" relationship is a necessary complement to the "Children of Adam" connection. The "Calamus" plant, a rare kind of Grass with "pink-tinged root" and "emblematic and capricious blades", appears as a phallic symbol of this exalted relationship. This comradeship would become the final cohering principle of the new world, the new Democracy—the perfect solidarity. This "manly love" is the final expression of the "Self":

> Come I will make the continent indissoluble,
>
> I will make the most splendid race the sun ever shone upon,
>
> I will make divine magnetic land, With the love of comrades,
>
> With the life-long love of Comrades...[21]

Thus Whitman believed that a male relationship was a necessary complement to a relationship with a woman and was required for the completion of the individual. Although critics have read the "Calamus" poems as a paean to homosexuality, there is no evidence that it is so. A purely sexual reading of the poems would merely reduce it to a chapter in auto-eroticism. "Calamus" was the result of the deepest convictions of Walt Whitman. Thus, acting from the last and profoundest centres, man is womanless. The continuation of the race is no longer in question. What we have is the sheer, ultimate being, the perfection of life, the polarity between man and man. In this final triumph of life, paradoxically, man comes close to death:

> Yet you are beautiful to me, you faint-tinged roots, you make me think of death;
>
> Death is beautiful from you (what, indeed, is finally beautiful except death and love?)
>
> I think it is not for life I am chanting here my chant of lovers,
>
> I think it must be for death...[22]

The "Calamus" element is responsible for the circuit of final friendship. This takes the "Self" away from the Woman to some place which is above and beyond. This is central to "Sea- Drift" where the male bird sings of the lost female. The female is not lost but merely lost to him who has to go beyond her. Thus the "Self" stands alone on the seashore of endless time, the last frontiers of life bringing the "Self" perilously close to death:

> Lip'd to me the low and delicious word death, And again death, death, death, death,
>
> Missing melodious, neither like the bird nor like my aroused Child's heart,
>
> But edging near as privately for me rustling at my feet,
>
> Creeping thence steadily up to my ears and loving me softly all over,
>
> Death, death, death, death, death...[23]

It is in the ultimate act of living and loving, which encompasses all men, that death is overcome. This is clearly evident in "whispers of heavenly death":

> O living always, always dying!
>
> O the burials of me past and present,
>
> O me while I stride ahead, material, visible impervious as ever
>
> O me, what I was for years, now dead (I lament not, I am content,)
>
> O to disengage myself from those corpses of me, which I turn and look to where I cast them,

> To pass on, (O living! always living!) and leave the corpses behind.[24]

Thus, the liberated "Self" overcomes death in a supreme assertion of self-hood:

> I was looking a long while for intentions, for a clue to the history of the past for myself and for these chants—and now I have found it,
>
> It is not in these paged fables in the libraries (them I neither accept nor reject)
>
> It is no more in the legends than in all else, It is in the present—it is this earth today,
>
> It is in Democracy—(the purpose and aim of all the past)
>
> It is the life of one man or one woman today—the average man of today...[25]

The 'Self' which Walt Whitman finally arrives at is the "Divine average," which basically implies an integration of the sublime and the commonplace. This was the essence of democracy, according to Whitman; further love was the universal leveller, the supreme qualizer.

D.H. Lawrence, more than any other critic, fathomed the vision of Whitman and his concept of the self. He states that "Whitman enters on the last phase of spiritual triumph. He really arrives at that stage of infinity, which the seers sought. By subjecting the deepest centres of the lower self, he attains the maximum consciousness in the higher self, a degree of intensive consciousness greater, perhaps, than any man in the modern world."[26] Like Lawrence's rediscovery of the "solar plexus", Whitman was able to unite in his concept of the 'Self' both the sublime and the erotic. His personal insights found him on the tract of the New Man as also the New World. His poetry highlighted the simple separate man, the "En-Masse" as against class poetry which represented the exceptional man. Whitman proposes to be the voice of democracy, a representative of the "Divine Average." Through the medium of the sense and unbounded love, Whitman came to believe in the brotherhood of man as a self-evident reality. His vision embraces America as well as the whole world.

End Notes

1. Van Wych Brooks, "The Precipitant", *Three Essays on America,* 1934 by E.P. Dutton and Co., Inc.
2. Anthony Burgess, "The Answerer", *Urgent Copy* (New York: W.N. Norton &. Co., 1968), 48-53.
3. Walt Whitman, *Notes and Fragments*, ed. R.M. Bucks (Folcraft, Pa: Flocrafts Press, 1899), Part II Item 1, 55.
4. "Song of Myself", Section 5, 33. Walt Whitman, *Leaves of Grass*, ed., Sculley Bradley, Harold W. Blodgett (New Delhi: Prentice Hall of India, 1986) (All references to poems are to this edition).
5. *Emerson Journals*, ed. E.W. Emerson and R.W. Forbes (New York, 1911), V, 380.
6. "Starting from Paul Mauok", Section 7.
7. *Leaves of Grass Inscriptions,* "Me Imperturbe", 11.
8. "Song of Myself" (Section 48), 87.
9. *Ibid.*, 87.
10. *Ibid.*, 73.
11. "D.H. Lawrence 'Whitman'", *Nation and Athenaeum*, XXIX (July 23, 1921), 616-18. Reprinted by permission of the New Statesman, London edition.
12. *Leaves of Grass* (Autumn Rivulets), 364.
13. "Children of Adam," "To the Garden of the World", *Leaves of Grass*, 90.
14. *Ibid.*, 96.
15. James E. Miller, *A Critical Guide to Leaves of Grass*, 41.
16. *Ibid.*, 96-97.
17. *Ibid.*, 101.
18. *Ibid.*, 93.
19. *Ibid.*, 391.
20. D.H. Lawrence, "The Birth of Sex", *Fantasia of the Unconscious.*
21. Calamus, 117 (*Leaves of Grass*).
22. *Leaves of Grass*, 114.
23. *Ibid.,* 253.
24. *Ibid.*, 24. 25. *Ibid.*, 387.
26. D.H. Lawrence (Sec. 11), 844.

Conclusion

> *There is a horror in things, a horror at the heart of the meaninglessness of existence. Some people cling to a certain philosophy that is handed down to them and which they accept. Life has a meaning if you're bucking for heaven. But if heaven is a fantasy, we are in this jungle with whatever we can work out for ourselves. It seems to me the cards are stacked against us.*
>
> "The World I Live In"
>
> —Tennessee Williams

This analysis explores the humanistic perspective in the writings of Emerson, Thoreau, Hawthorne, and Melville; a perspective evident in their respective attitude towards man. This attitude finds expression in transcendental terms in Emerson, in romantic naturalist terms in Thoreau, in psychological terms in Hawthorne and Melville and finally in prophetic terms in Whitman; taken collectively, it would imply "The Song of Man."

Critical evaluations of nineteenth-century American Literature highlight the unique features of the age, which include its transcendental bias and the emergence of the psychological novel. It was a period which F.O. Matthiessen called the "American Renaissance" and which historians likewise classified as "American Romanticism." The introductory chapter explores the unique humanism of the age, which was reflected in literature written during the period. In the dissertation, an attempt has been made to explore the socio-historical factors at work which were directly responsible for this anthropocentric vision. These contributory factors include "the American Dream", "Expansion and Self-trust", and the reorientation of literature under the influence of New England transcendentalism.

The five American writers referred to above were alive to the problems that beset man as man. They were also aware of his immense potential. Further, the humanistic perspective in their writings was radically universalized. The emphasis was not on man as European or American but on man freed from the accidents of time and space. A second assumption common to the five writers is that the key to human happiness lies in self-realization, *i.e.* a harmonious blending of the egoistic and altruistic motivations in the self. While Emerson, Thoreau and Whitman realize this ideal, Hawthorne and Melville are not so convinced that a genuine harmony between man and the universe is possible.

The discussion on Emerson explores through his writings his unique vision of man. Keeping in mind his transcendental bias, "Man" is basically the transcendental man. Key concepts discussed include Emerson's concept of "Self", self-reliance and non-conformity. In addition, Emerson gives significance to the triangular relation between Man, Nature and the Oversoul. Finally, the central thrust of Emerson's exploration of man is his assumption that whatever truth lies beyond or outside man can only be reached through him and by himself.

Thoreau as a romantic naturalist abjured all codified ties with society and the universe. Having become dissociated with Nature, Thoreau saw man as working his way back to his natural center, re-establishing his lost rapport with Nature. He saw man as developing an organic relationship with Nature. The discussion on Thoreau keeps in mind the fact that man should be in perfect correspondence with Nature: "at home with Nature."

Barriss Mills in his essay "Hawthorne and Puritanism", traces back to Hawthorne's Puritan ancestry two of the most insistent themes of his fiction—the universal depravity of man and the humanising effect of sin. Thus the discussion on Hawthorne keeps in mind his psychological bent of mind, his exploration of the inner landscape of the mind and soul. His novels and short stories used the case histories of men and women afflicted by guilt or, as he called it, "a stain upon the soul." An attempt has been made to study the characters of Hawthorne as psychological portraits of people confronted with the problem of good and evil. In the ultimate analysis, Hawthorne seems convinced about the regenerative power of sin.

While Hawthorne settles for a compromise between Man and the universe, Herman Melville is obdurate; his is an "everlasting No." Man and Nature are seen in an eternal conflict and ceaseless destruction. Like Hawthorne, the characters of Melville grapple with the problem of good and evil, but the "Mystery of iniquity" is never solved. Man and Nature remain forever antithetical.

The fatalistic streak which colours Hawthorne and Melville is nowhere found in Whitman. The discussion on Whitman emphasizes the fact that his was a glorious celebration, a prophetic awareness of man. Whitman did not seek to highlight the exceptional man, rather, he proposed to be the voice of democracy, a representative of the "divine average." The emphasis in the chapter on Whitman is on his passionate argument heralding the dawn of a new man, a new society, a new hope, a road each must travel for himself. The new man has to relocate his intellectual culture to new sources of power, in the beautiful blood, in the ardours of sex, in a new harmony like that of animals with the physical universe.

As is evident, the humanistic perspective in the writings of Emerson, Thoreau, Hawthorne, Melville and Whitman qualify their man-centered or anthropocentric vision of the universe—epitomising in a nutshell, their "Song of Man." Without denying the existence of God or brute matter, man and his world are explained as far as possible in terms of man himself. The transcendentalists believed that the structure of the universe duplicates the structure of the individual self. Thus, all knowledge stems from self-knowledge. Hawthorne and Melville likewise dwelt upon the allegory of human experience. Thoreau postulated an organic relation between man and the universe, in consonance with the natural rhythms of life. Whitman likewise felt that every man freed from the accidents of space and time forms part of a physical and spiritual continuum.

Finally, in conclusion, it would be well to place the five American writers in perspective. If Emerson, Thoreau and Whitman represented the affirmative aspect of American romanticism, Hawthorne and Melville represented its sceptical questioning side. Thus, any analysis of the five writers brings in its wake the makings of the great American Nation—the socio-historical process at work. The 'American Dream' culminated in a paean to man, a glorious celebration of man— the Song of Man. This fact is amply qualified by the American Renaissance and the nineteenth-century writers of American literature. But there appears to be an exception to this rule, an anomaly exists in the writings of Edgar Allan Poe. His works provide a watershed, a turning point. Any discussion of the nineteenth-century attitude towards man would be incomplete without a brief reference to this factor. Poe was at odds with his time; his works are a pointer to the future, to the gradual corruption of the American dream.

Edward Stone shows how Poe's discovery of "our great subject, the disintegration of the modern personality" and his preoccupation with the theme of "the sickness of mind" and "despair at the universe" makes his works "the very fable of our existence."[1] Poe looks forward to the twentieth century, to the concerns of Eliot, Fitzgerald, Hemingway and Faulkner. The evil to which Emerson was impervious finds its way into the cosmopolitan dilemma of Henry James. Man in the modern context is dislocated and lost in a moral and social vacuum. Perhaps the most important feature of modern American literature, which distinguishes it from nineteenth-century literature, is the overhanging gloom of pessimism. Modern American dramatists present the world as purposeless and chaotic to the point that evil exists beyond the individual's ability to control it. Man is no longer the master of his destiny. The works of Arthur Miller and Eugene O'Neill are mere attempts to impart some pattern to the chaotic flux.

The modern critique of man thus implies a shift of focus primarily. The modernists look to the "futility and anarchy" of the world to explain man. This is unlike the nineteenth-century writers of American literature who turned to the man to effect a cosmos out of chaos. Emerson, Thoreau, Hawthorne, Melville, and Whitman delved into the enigma posed by Man. They concluded alike that man was the measure of their radically anthropocentric vision of the world.

End Notes

1. Edward Stone, "Poe in and out of his Time" is reprinted from *Emerson Society Quarterly*, XXXI (II Quarter 1963), 14-17.

Select Bibliography

Abel, Darrel, *The Moral Picturesque: Studies in Hawthorne's fiction*. Indiana: Pardue University Press, 1985.

Adams, Stephen and Donald Ross, Jr., *Revising Mythologies: The composition of Thoreau's major works*. Charlottesville: University of Virginia Press, 1988.

Alcott, Amos Bronson, *Ralph Waldo Emerson, Philosopher and Seer: An estimate of his character and genius in prose and verse*. Boston: Cuppless and Hurd, 1888.

Asselineau, Roger, *Merrill Studies in the House of Seven Gables*. Ohio: Merrill, 1970.

Barish, Evelyn, *Emerson: The roots of prophecy*. Princeton: Princeton University Press, 1989.

Baym, Nina, *The Scarlet Letter: A reading*. Boston: Twayne Publishers, 1986.

Bishop, Jonathan, *Emerson on the Soul*. Massachussetts: Harvard University Press, 1964.

Bloom, Harold Ed., *Herman Melville's Moby-Dick*. New York: Chelsea House Publishers, 1986.

Bloom, Harold Ed., *Nathaniel Hawthorne*. New York: Chelsea House Publishers, 1986.

Bloom, Harold Ed., *Ahab*. New York: Chelsea House Publishers, 1991.

Borst, Raymond R., *A Descriptive Bibliography*. Pittsburgh: University of Pittsburgh, 1982.

Boswell, Jeanette, *Herman Melville and the Critics: A checklist of criticism 1900-1978*. N.J. Scarecrow Press, 1981.

Bowen, Merlin, *Self and Experience in the Writings of Herman Melville*. Chicago: The University of Chicago Press, 1960.

Brauch, Watson G. Ed., *Melville: The critical heritage*. London: Routeledge and Kegan Paul, 1974.

Bredahl, A. Carl, *Melville's Angles of Vision*. Gainsville: University of Florida Press, 1972.

Bridges, William E., *Spokesman for the Self: Emerson, Thoreau, Whitman*. Scranton: Chandler, 1971.

Brodhead, Richard H., *Hawthorne, Melville and the Novel.*

Chicago: University of Chicago Press, 1976.

Brodhead, Richard H. Ed., *New Essays on Moby-Dick or the Whale*. Cambridge: Cambridge University Press, 1986.

Bucke, Richard Maurice, *Cosmic Consciousness: A study in the evolution of the human mind*. New York: University Books, 1961.

Burkholder, Robert E. and Joel Myerson, *Critical Essays on Ralph Waldo Emerson*. Massachussetts: G.K. Hall and Co., 1983.

Cady, H. and Louis J. Budd Ed., *On Walt Whitman: The best from American Literature*. Durham: Duke University Press, 1987.

Cady, Edwin and Loius J. Budd, *On Melville*. Cady: Duke University Press, 1988.

Cameron, Kenneth Walter, *Emerson and Thoreau as Readers: Selected chapters from the Transcendentalists and Minerva*. Hartford: Transcendental Books, 1958.

Cameron, Kenneth Walter, *Transcendental Climate: New resources for the study of Emerson, Thoreau and their contemporaries*. Hartford: Transcendental Books, 1963.

Cameron, Kenneth Walter, *Hawthorne Index to Themes, Motifs, Topics, Archetypes, Sources and Key Words Dealt with in Recent Criticism*. Hartford: Transcendental Books, 1968.

Carlisle, E. Fred, *The Uncertain Self: Whitman's drama of identity*. East Cansing: Michigan State University Press, 1973.

Carpenter, Frederic Ives, *Emerson Handbook*. New York: Hendricks House Inc., 1953.

Cavell, Stanley, *The Senses of Walden*. San Francisco: North Point Press, 1981.

Cavitch, David, *My Soul and I: The inner life of Walt Whitman*. Boston: Beaton Press, 1985.

Chary, V.K. Allen, Gay Wilson (Introd), *Whitman in the Light of Vedantic Mysticism: An appreciation*. Lincoln: University of Nebraska Press, 1964.

Chase, Richard Ed., *A Collection of Critical Essays*. Englewood Cliffs: Prentice Hall, 1962.

Clarke, Ceadie Mac, *Walt Whitman's Concept of the American Common Man*. New York: Philosophica Library, 1955.

Cook, Reginald Lansing, *Passage to Walden*. Boston: Houghton, 1949.

Cowan, Bainard, *Eniled Walers: Moby-Dick and the crises of allegory*. Baton Rouge: Louisiana State University Press, 1982.

Crawley, Thomas Edward, *The Structure of the 'Leaves of Grass'*. Austin: University of Texas Press, 1970.

Crowley, J. Donald Ed., *Hawthorne: The crititical heritage*.

London: Routledge and Kegan Paul, 1970.

Davis, Merrell Ress, *Melville's 'Mardie': A chartless voyage*.

Hamden: Archon Books, 1967.

De Selincourt, Basil, *Walk Whitman: A critical study*. New York: Russell, 1965.

Doren, Mark Van, *The Portable Emerson*. New York: Viking, 1946.

Doren, Mark Van, *Nathaniel Hawthorne*. Minneapolis: University of Minnesota Press, 1992.

Duncan, Jeffrey L., *The Power and Form of Emerson Thought*.

Charlo Hesville: University Press of Virginia, 1973.

Ellis, Havelock, *The New Spirit*. London: Walter Scott, 1892.

Erlich, Gloria C., *Family Themes and Hawthorne's Fiction: The tenacious web*. N.J.: Rutgers University Press, 1986.

Fausset, Hugh J'anson, *Walt Whitman: Poet of democracy*. New York: Haskell House, Publishers of Scholarly Books, 1966.

Fenn, Mary Gail, *Thoreau's Rivers*: Concord Massachusetts.

N.Y.: Thoreau Society Inc., 1973.

Fishwick, Marshall W., *Common Culture and the Great Tradition: The case for renewal*. Connecticut: Greenwood Press, 1982.

Fogle, Richard Harter, *Hawthorne's Fiction: The light and the dark*. Norman: University of Oklahama Press, 1952.

Fogle, Richard Harter, *Melville's Shorter Tales*. Norman: University of Oklahama Press, 1970.

Franklin, H. Bruce, *The Wake of the Gods: Melville's mythology*. Stanford: Stanford University Press, 1963.

Gay, Robert Malcolm, *Emerson: A study of the poet as seer*.

New York: Doubleday, 1928.

Gerber, John C. Ed., *Twentieth Century Interpretations of the Scarlet Letter: A collection of critical essays*. Englewood Cliffs: Prentice-Hall, 1968.

Gonnaud, Maurice, *An Uneasy Solitude: Individual and society in the work of Ralph Waldo Emerson*. Princeton: Princeton University Press, 1987.

Graebner, Norman A., *Manifest Destiny*. New York: The Bobb Merrill Company Inc., 1968.

Gray, Henry David, *Emerson: A statement of New England Transcendentalism as expressed in the philosophy of its chief exponent*. New York: Ungar, 1958.

Hansen, Olaf, *Aesthetic Individualism and Practical Intellect: American allegory in Emerson, Thoreau, Adams, and James*. New Jersey: Princeton University Press, 1990.

Harding, Walter Roy Ed., *Thoreau: A century of criticism*.

Dallas: Southern Methodist University Press, 1954.

Harding, Walter Roy, *A Thoreau Handbook*. New York: New York University Press, 1959.

Harding, Walter Roy, *Henry David Thoreau's Walden and Civil Disobedience: A study guide*. N.J: Shelley Publishing Company, 1962.

Harding, Walter Roy, *Emerson's Library*. Charlorresvilles: University Press of Virginia, 1967.

Hartz, Louis, *The Liberal Tradition in America*. New York: Harcourt, Brace and Company, 1955.

Hazard, Arthur, *Man the Measure: An essay on humanism as religion*. Princeton: Princeton University Press, 1939.

Herbert, T. Walter Jr., *Moby-Dick and Calvinism: A world dismantled*. New Brunswick: Rutgers University Press, 1977.

Hildebidle, John, *Thoreau: A naturalist's liberty*. Mass: Harvard University Press, 1933.

Hillway, Tyrus, *Herman Melville*. Boston: Twayne Publishers, 1979.

Hindus, Milton Ed., *Leaves of Grass: One hundred years after*. Stanford: Stanford University Press, 1955.

Howard, Leon, *Pamphlets on American Writers: Herman Melville*. Minneapolis: University of Minnesota Press, 1961.

Howarth, William L., *The Book of Concord: Thoreau's life as a writer*. Harmondsworth: Penguin Books, 1983.

James, Henry, *Hawthorne*. London: MacMillan, 1883.

James, Laurie, *Men, Women and Margaret Fuller: The truth that existed between Margaret Fuller and Ralph Waldo Emerson and their circle of Transcendental friends*. New York: Golden Heritage Press, 1990.

Jehlan, Myra, *American Incarnation: The individual, the nation and the continent*. Massachussetts: Harvard University Press, 1986.

Kesterson, David B., *The Merrill Studies in 'The Marble Faun'*. Ohio: Merrill, 1971.

Kesterson, David B., *Critical Essays on Hawthorne's 'The Scarlet Letters'*. Boston: G.K. Hall and Co., 1988.

Krieg, Joan P., *Walt Whitman: Here and now*. Westport; Greenwood Press, 1985.

Krutch, Joseph Wood, *Henry Davis Thoreau*. New York: William Sloane Associates, 1948.

Kuebrich, David, *Minor Prophecy: Walt Whitman's New American Religion*. Bloomington: Indiana University Press, 1989.

Kurtz, Paul Ed., *The Humanistic Alternative: Some definitions of humanism*. New York: Prometheus Books, 1973.

Lee, A. Robert, *Nathaniel Hawthorne: New critical essays*.

London: Vision Press Ltd., 1982.

Levin, Harry, *The Power of Blackness: Hawthorne, Poe, Melville*. New York: Vintage Books, 1960.

Marinacci, Barbara, *O Wondrous Singer!* New York: Dodd, Mead and Co., 1970.

Matthiessen, Francis Otto, *American Renaissance: Art and expression in the age of Emerson and Whitman*. London: Oxford University Press, 1941.

McCarthy, Paul, *The Twisted Mind: Madness in Herman Melville's fiction*. Iowa City: University of Iowa Press, 1990.

McIntosh, James, *Thoreau as Romantic Naturalist: His shifting stance towards nature*. Ithaca: Cornell University Press, 1974.

McPherson, *Hugo, Hawthorne as Myth-Maker: A study in imagination*. Toronto: University of Toronto Press, 1969.

Miller, Edwin Haviland Ed., *A Country of Whitman Criticism*.

Bloomington: Indiana University Press, 1969.

Miller, James E., Shapiro Karl, Jt. Auth Slote, Bernice Jt. Auth, *Start with the Sun: Studies in cosmic poetry*. Lincoln: University of Nebraska Press, 1960.

Miller, James E., *A Reader's Guide to Herman Melville*. New York: Farrar, 1962.

Miller, James E., *Walt Whitman*. New York: Twayne Publishers, 1962.

Miller, Perry Ed., *The American Transcendentalists: Their prose and poetry*. New York: Doubleday Anchor Books, 1957.

Mott, Wesley T., *The Strains of Eloquence: Emerson and his sermon*. University Park: Pennsylvania State University Press, 1989.

Mulder, Robert (Intro), *Critical Essays on Melville's Billy Budd, Sailor*. Boston: G.K. Hall and Co., 1989.

Murray, James G., *Great American Thinkers: Henry David Thoreau*. New York: Washington Square Press, 1968.

Myerson, Joel, *Emerson Century Essays*. Carbondale: Southern Illinois University Press, 1982.

Myerson, Joel, *Critical Essays on Henry David Thoreau's Walden*. Bosten: G.K. Hall and Co., 1988.

Olson, Charles, *Call Me Ishmael: A study of Melville*. New York: Reynol and Hitchcock, 1947.

Paul, Sherman, *Emerson's Angle of Vision: Man and nature in the American Experience*. Massa: Harvard University Press, 1952.

Paul, Sherman Ed., *Thoreau: A collection of critical essays*. Engelewood Cliffs: Prentice-Hall, 1962.

Pelleg, Angelo, *An Immigrant's Quest: American dream*. San Francisco: North Point Press, 1986.

Person, Leland S., *Aesthetic Headaches: Woman and a masculine poetics in Poe, Melville and Hawthorne*. Athens: University of Georgia Press, 1988.

Porte, Joel, *Emerson and Thoreau: Transcendentalist in conflict*. Conn: Weslayan University Press, 1966.

Porte, Joel, *Transcendentalists in Conflict*. Middletown: Wesleyan University Press, 1966.

Porter, David, *Emerson and Literary Change*. Massachussetts: Harvard University Press, 1978.

Sharpiro, Charles Ed., *Twelve Original Essays on Great American Novels*. Detroit: Wayne: State University Press, 1958.

Sowder, William J., *Emerson's Reviews and Commentators: A biographical and bibliographical criticism with a detailed index*. Hartford: Transcendental Books, 1968.

Stafford, William T., *Melville's 'Billy Budd' and the Critics*.

Belmont: Wadsworth Publishing Co., 1961.

Stein, William Bysshe, *Hawthorne's Faust: A study of the devil archetype*. Hamden: Archon Books, 1968.

Stoehr, Taylor, *Hawthorne's Mad Scientists: Pseudoscience and social science in nineteenth century life and letters*. Hamden: Archon Books, 1978.

Strauch, Carl F., *Characteristics of Emerson: Transcendental poet, a symposium*. Hartford: Transcendental Books, 1975.

Taylor, J. Golden, *Hawthorne's Ambivalence towards Puritanism*. Utah State University Press, 1965.

Thompson, Lawarence R., *Melville's Quarrel with God*. Princeton: Princeton University Press, 1952.

Van Cromphout, Gustaaf, *Emerson's Modernity and the Example of Goethe*. Columbia: University of Missouri Press, 1990.

Van Doren, Mark, *Nathaniel Hawthorne*. New York: Sloane, 1949.

Van Doren, Mark, *Henry David Thoreau: A Critical Study*. New York: Russell, 1961.

Waggoner, Hyatt H., *Nathaniel Hawthorne*. Minneapolis: University of Minnesota Press, 1962.

Waggoner, Hyatt H., *Emerson as Poet*. Princeton: Princeton University Press, 1974.

Woodress, James, *Critical Essays on Walt Whitman*. Boston: Hall, 1983.

Index